PSYCHO-SOCIAL ASPECTS OF DOMESTIC VIOLENCE

About the Author

Dr. Sushma Pandey, is a Reader in Psychology at D.D.U. Gorakhpur University, Gorakhpur. Earlier, she has served in the Department of Population Studies, S.V. University, Tirupati. Her areas of interest include Social Psychology, Community Psychology, Cognitive and Developmental Processes.

Dr. Pandey has worked extensively in the fields of child abuse, domestic violence, women empowerment, reproductive health, stress and coping. She has published numerous research articles in the national and international journals of repute. She has recently published a book titled, *Psychological Consequences of Child Abuse.*

Dr. Pandey has completed two major research projects entitled, *"Social Dynamics of Child Abuse and its Psychological Consequences in Eastern Districts of U.P."* **and** *"Psycho-Social Dynamics of Domestic Violence and Its Impact on Children,"* **Also she has completed nine research projects under D.S.A. Programme. Currently, she is working on intervention strategies to prevent child abuse, domestic violence and their consequences.**

Psycho-Social Aspects of DOMESTIC VIOLENCE

Sushma Pandey

CONCEPT PUBLISHING COMPANY, NEW DELHI-110 059

Cataloging in Publication Data—DK
Courtesy: D.K. Agencies (P) Ltd. <docinfo@dkagencies.com>

Pandey, Sushma, 1959-
Pyscho-social aspects of domestic violence / Sushma Pandey.
p. cm.
Study conducted at rural and urban areas of Gorakhpur region of Uttar Pradesh, India.
Includes bibliographical references (p.).
Includes index.
ISBN 13: 9788180695339
ISBN 10: 8180695336

1. Family violence—India—Gorakhpur Region—Psychological aspects. 2. Women--Violence against—India—Gorakhpur Region. 3. Child abuse—India—Gorakhpur Region I. Title.

DDC 362.829 209 542 22

ISBN-13: 978-81-8069-533-9
ISBN-10: 81-8069-533-6

First Published 2008

Published and Printed by
Ashok Kumar Mittal
Concept Publishing Company
A/15-16, Commercial Block, Mohan Garden
New Delhi-110 059 (INDIA)

Phones : 25351460, 25351794
Fax : 091-11-25357103
Email : publishing@conceptpub.com

Foreword

Women represent almost half of the world's population. They contribute to human economic activities in many significant ways. As home makers and child care takers they have always occupied a prominent place in human society. Over the years they have also come forward to participate in the new economic lives that require them to move out of the premises of the house in which they remained confined until a few decades ago. Today they are represented almost in all walks of life, although the representation is fairly selective, numerically weak and also sometimes uneven. This is especially true in developing countries where a majority of the women still remain bound with age-old traditions that do not allow them to participate in and take advantage of education, health and other developmental opportunities.

Psychological studies of women have globally proliferated during the last few decades. These studies have focused not only on the perception of women by men (and by other women), but also on the ways in which they are discriminated against and harassed by the members of the society at large. As a result, violence against women has become a major concern of social-psychological thinking and research, nationally as well as internationally. Since any form of violence brings severe consequences for physical and mental health of women, the World Health Organization developed a special agenda for the study of violence-related health problems of women about a decade ago. Guided by this initiative, several studies have been carried out during the last one decade that focus on topics like physical, sexual and psychological violence occurring in the family and in the general community (including battering), dowry-related violence, rape, non-spousal violence and violence related to exploitation, sexual harassment and intimidation at work, in educational institutions and elsewhere, trafficking in women, forced prostitution, and sexual abuse of children.

These studies have led to the search of pathways of the violence against women. It in indicated that violence against women results from a combination of individual biological and psychological characteristics as well as social, economic and political factors. Certain working models have been developed for comprehending the dynamics of violence by focusing on *individual, interpersonal, institutional* and *structural* factors. These models demonstrate how the interaction of individual and social characteristics can constitute protective or risk factors that shape the nature and consequences of violence, but they fall short of explaining violence related phenomena in the multi-cultural mosaic of the Indian society.

Given this state of affairs the present monograph on "Psycho-Social Aspects of Domestic Violence" by Dr. Sushma Pandey appears to be highly welcoming academic effort. As a keen researcher Dr. Pandey has attempted to capture a number of issues pertaining to domestic violence. Considering it as the most pervasive form of violence she attempts to trace the patterns of domestic violence in relation to a number of contextual and psychological variables. The study indicates that domestic violence and related behavioural phenomena are rooted in the socio-economic and familial conditions of women, in both rural and urban settings. That the psychological characteristics of individuals are linked in important ways to the socio-economic and cultural conditions in which they are placed is not something new that this study informs us about. On the other hand, the patterns of relationships demonstrated among variables in the study carry enough potential to suggest social psychologists to develop intervention programs for dealing with the problems of domestic violence. The study brings out clearly that domestic violence has several negative consequences for children who are exposed to it directly or indirectly. If children constitute the precious wealth of a nation that has to be saved, psychologists will have to come forward to help the society in developing protective measures against domestic violence.

This monograph contains a wealth of information. Hence, it is likely that readers find it slightly over occupied with presentation of data sets and use of statistical overtones. However, I strongly hope that the monograph will serve two important purposes for the community of psychologists. In the first place, it will stimulate researchers to understand the nature and correlates of domestic violence and help them in designing research studies that probe deeper into its complex dynamics. Secondly, it will help psychologists and other social scientists, interested in human welfare, to design intervention programs for the prevention of violence in families and rehabilitation of children who have been the victims of domestic violence.

R.C. Mishra
Professor of Psychology
Banaras Hindu University
Varanasi-221 005

Preface

Domestic violence as a socio-psychological construct is fraught with ubiquity. Over the last few decades, issues related to domestic violence have received widespread attention in public and professionals understanding. It is now realized that 'violence against women, is epidemic in our society since antiquity and is gradually threatening the very existence of women community in particular and humanity in general.

Primarily, domestic violence emerged as a social issue in developed countries (Starus, Galles & Steinmetz., 1980) however, it was realized that it exists in same form or other in developing countries like India at alarming volume. Although, preventive services have been proliferated in developed countries, however, except legal enforcements, no significant effort has been made to eradicate this evil from our society. Despite this, without understanding the causative roots of domestic violence and its consequences on children and family, preventive efforts can not be made successfully.

This issue struck to my mind a few years ago, when I was engaged with field work for my earlier research project on "Social Dynamics of Child Abuse and Its Psychological Consequences in Eastern Districts of U.P.". During the household data collection, I witnessed a numerable number of women living in very pathetic condition. In traditional families, women are not given opportunity to participate in decision making on most personal issues including personal health and children's career. Apart from this, they are abused and harassed in many ways. Preferably, girls are found more abused than boys in the family. I continued witnessing such events in my surrounding and identified raising graph of Domestic Violence with the passage of time. Meanwhile, National Commission for Women (NCW) provided an opportunity to design a research study on women problems. Fortunately, I availed this opportunity to conduct a research study on, "Psycho-Social Dynamics of Domestic Violence and Its Impact on Children".

I identified rural and urban areas of Gorakhpur district for the setting of research study, since this district is densely populated, underdeveloped and different forms of domestic violence against women and children are reported very often. Surprisingly, this problem is not limited to only low strata families but is also present in each and every strata of society with little variations in magnitude and forms of abuses. This research study investigated the role of social and psychological factors in the origin and sustenance of domestic violence and its impact on children. Findings of the study evinced surprising facts and a numerable number of issues have been raised on the basis of present results.

This monograph entitled, *"Psycho-Social Aspects of Domestic Violence"* consists of five major chapters. In the first chapter, the conceptualization of domestic violence, its incidence and prevalence rate in India and worldwide, causative factors and consequences of domestic violence on emergence of child abuse and behavioural dysfunctions in children, have been systematically reported. The objectives and hypotheses of the study have also been derived on the basis of pertinent literature, mentioned in this chapter. Chapter II deals with plans, strategy and procedure of the study. The statistical treatment of data and obtained results have been recorded in Chapter III. This chapter also includes a set of 12 case histories of abused women victims of domestic violence. In the 4th Chapter, findings of the study have been interpreted and discussed with the support of empirical and theoretical evidences. Further, in the fifth chapter conclusion of the study have been reported on the basis of present findings, a theoretical framework has been developed by the investigator to pinpoint the psycho-social dynamics of domestic violence and its consequences lastly, tentative recommendations have been made on the basis of present study. Though, researcher is aware of the limitations of this piece of research and does not assert that this research is a pioneering effort to investigate the role of socio-psychological factors in the origin, prevalence and consequences of domestic violence. Despite this, findings of the study recommend for urgent preventive interventions to both perpetrators (Abusers) and abused victims (women and children). The investigator sincerely feels the need for designing innovative intervention programmes to aware families and public about the damaging consequences of domestic violence on development and well-being of women and children. Present piece of study has raised many more questions which are still unresolved, however, finding of the study will provide a strong base to investigate such issues in further researches and design innovative intervention programmes to aware women, family and the larger society.

Sushma Pandey

Acknowledgements

It is with a great sense of gratitude that I acknowledge the guidance and support, which I received from inception to completion of this research project. Since this investigation was carried out with the financial assistance provided by the National Commission for Women (NCW), New Delhi, thus, I express my sincere gratitude to the organization for timely support to complete the project without any difficulty.

During the conduction of this study, I consulted and received guidance, support and encouragements from a number of renowned senior psychologists. First of all, I express my sincere gratitude to Prof. L.B. Tripathi, Former Head and Dean (Arts), D.D.U. Gorakhpur University for his persistent support, invaluable suggestions and guidance throughout the period. I am also grateful to Prof. (Mrs.) A. Agrawal, Ex Head, and other members of the Department of Psychology, D.D.U. Gorakhpur University for their suggestions and encouragements.

I consulted and received suggestions and supports from many academicians of other universities amongst whom the names of Prof. R.C. Tripathi, Director, G.B. Pant Social Science Institute, Allahabad, Prof. K. Mahadevan, Former Head and Dean, S.V. University, Tirupati, Prof. R.C. Mishra of B.H.U., Prof. Girishwar Mishra, and Prof. Anand Prakash, of Delhi University, Prof. S.N. Rai of Meerut University, Prof. Mukta Rani Rastogi and Prof. P.C. Mishra, of Lucknow University, Prof. K.N. Tripathi of Bhopal University, my father Sri Ram Adhar Tiwari (Retired Lecturer and versatile Reader), Ballia District and Mr. Vibhava Prakash Tripathi, Senior Advocate, High Court, Allahabad need special gratitudes.

I extend my heartfelt thanks to my husband Dr. R.N. Pandey, Reader in Economics, my parents and my children

(Avanish and Rishabh). They have been constant sources of motivation and pillars of support throughout the period.

I am also thankful to Mrs. Sangeeta Pandey, Counsellor Family Court, Gorakhpur for providing valuable information and supports, whenever I needed.

I extend thanks to my students and the Project team: Dr. Saurabh Kr. Tiwari, Mr. Sunil Kumar Mishra, Miss Manjari Singh, Mr. Abhay Pratap Singh and Mr. Pragyesh Kumar Mishra, Anurakti Chaturvedi (R.S.) who worked silently with great devotion throughout the period.

Last but not the least, I must be thankful to all the Respondents (women and children), who participated in this research study. I also extent my thanks to Mr. S.K. Shukla for typing the report and transforming it into the presentable shape.

Sushma Pandey

Contents

List of Tables

List of Figures

1

Introduction

Domestic violence is a socio-psychological phenomenon, which is increasing at epidemic rate throughout the world and has challenged the very existence of human race in general and female population in particular. Over the last few decades, the domestic violence related issues have inflamed Women Organizations of both Government and Non-government cells and Feminists. On 8th March, 1984, an autonomous women's group across the country celebrated International Women's Day and focused on the theme of violence against women and major emphasis was given on domestic violence in the forms of bride burning/dowry deaths, infanticide, foeticide, sexual harassment, and wife battering etc. Consequently, various laws were framed and enforced during the last 20 years. Despite this, the rate of perpetrators and abused victims is dramatically increasing day by day and endangering the survival of a large segment of population.

Primarily, domestic violence emerged as a social issue in U.S.A. when Murray Straus and his colleagues (1980) completed their pioneering research for the book, "Behind Closed Doors: Violence in American Families." Afterwards, prolific researches from different perspectives were done in western countries. Researchers have shown their concern and are actively engaged to explore its prevalence rate, root causes and consequences, both social and psychological (Flavia, 1988; Ghadially, 1988; Jaffe, et. al., 2003; Pandey & Misra, 2000). Numerous preventive efforts have been proliferated in developed countries, however, such efforts are meager in developing countries like India.

Although, in India, domestic violence is found since antiquity. Women have been and are still maltreated in many ways (Manasa, Vaacha and Karmana) and they are bound to live in a pathetic state, yet the concept of 'Ardhanarishwar' (symbolizing the sense of balance or gender equity) is identified in Indian mythology. This is rather paradoxical where it is stated, "Yatra Naryastu Pujyante Ramante Tatra Devata", there are various forms of crimes against women committed by male counterparts.

The distress of women is also reflected in the following lines of Janabai (1298-1350):

> *"Let me not be sad because I am born a woman,*
> *In this world, many saints suffer in this way"*

(Janabai, 1298-1350)

A huge amount of such narratives are witnessed in the literature as well as cases around the world, and each tragic episode evinces the prevalence of overt and covert forms of domestic violence which are either unnoticed or ignored, considering them most personal or familial issues (Bhattacharya, 2004). The violences behind closed doors are found in all strata of society in India and other countries too. According to WHO report on Domestic Violence and Health (2002), it is assumed that interpersonal violence results in the fatality (deaths) of one person every minute somewhere across the world. Similarly, World Development Report—suggests that domestic violence and rapes occur at the rate of 5 per cent of the total disease burden amongst women in the larger group between 15 to 44 years. Apart from this, police records present the statistics of crimes against women in India ; Women are sexually abused (raped) every 34 minutes, molested every 26 minutes, kidnapped every 43 minutes and killed every 93 minutes. Thus, violence against women continues to be a global epidemic that kills, harasses, tortures and abuses—physically, sexually, psychologically and economically. The domestic violence against women is witnessed in every country cutting across boundaries of caste, community, ethnicity, culture, age, income, education and occupation. No society can claim to be free of such violence, the only difference is in its patterns and trends that exists in countries and regions. Despite this, specific groups of women are more vulnerable including minority, indigenous, migrants, institutionalized or women with disabilities, elderly women, poor or low S.E.S. women and female children respectively. While reliable statistics of domestic violence are hard to identify, however, studies estimate that from nation to nation 20 to 50 per cent of women have experienced physical and sexual harassments and mental torture or psychological abuses (UNICEF, 2000). No doubt, this evil is epidemic in our country. The causes of domestic violence are multifaceted and its consequences are damaging. Therefore, it was considered essential to investigate the socio-psychological causative roots of domestic violence and its impact on children who are exposed to violences behind closed doors.

Conceptualization of Domestic Violence

The domestic violence is conceptualized as, "one intimate partner's (spouse) attempt to control, dominate and humiliate the other partner through a variety of means viz; physical, sexual, psychological, economic and spiritual abuse. Domestic violence goes beyond individual acts of aggression to encompass an overall pattern of behaviour aimed at maintaining full control over the partner" (Jaffe *et al.,* 2003). The National Research Council (1993) defined, "Domestic violence is the intentional infliction of harm or injury by one intimate partner on another" (National Research Council, 1993).

Researchers and professionals have identified that domestic violence escalates in both frequency and severity over time and without intervention, battering may grow into a habitual way of resolving family conflicts. Murray, Straus and his colleagues (1980) were the first social scientists to confirm what the women's movement and battered women's shelter advocates had sometimes pointed out that, "Home was not a safe place." This research uncovered the fact that millions of men, women and children lived with violence as an integral part of family life.

Apart from this, from legal perspective domestic violence is defined as; "The physical injury, sexual abuse or forced imprisonment or threat of a family or household member or of a minor child by a person with whom the minor child has had or is having a dating relationship."

From Socio-Psychological perspective it is viewed that domestic violence can occur in the variety of relationship including same sex relationships, extended family relationships, dating, acquaintance and peer relationship. Domestic violence takes place across all groups and cultures. Patterns of violent behaviour can be transmitted from one generation to the next. Thus, domestic violence or women abuse is a widespread societal problem. It is a form of power and control. It affects the physical, social, emotional and financial well-being of women and children. It can take many forms, including verbal, emotional, psychological, financial, spiritual, sexualand physical abuses. Women from all racial and ethnic backgrounds, sexual orientations, socio-economic classes, religions, ability levels and professions have experienced abuse in their lifetime.

Epidemiology and Forms of Domestic Violence (DV)

World wide prevalence rate of domestic violence indicates that females are more abused than males. According to Straus *et al.'s* research report, 1 out of 10 women had confirmed violence at the hands of the one, they loved and three per cent (3%) experienced severe violence including life threatening attacks and injuries.

In 1984, the Department of Attorney General disclosed domestic violence a major social problem that if tolerated allows the seeds of violence to be sown in the next generation. Further in 1992, the American Medical Association reported that women were four times more likely to be injured in their homes by their partners than in any vehicle accidents (American Medical Association, 1992).

According to the U.S. National Violence Against Women Survey (Tjaden & Thoennes, 2000), 22 per cent of the women and 7.4 per cent of the men surveyed reported that they were physically assaulted by their partners. As estimated, 1.3 million woman and 835,000 men are physically assaulted by their intimate partner in U.S.

Similarly, statistics from Australia also confirm high rate of domestic violence. The Australian Bureau of Statistics reports that 23 per cent of women experienced violence by an intimate partner in their lifetime (Putt & Higgins, 1997), 12 per cent of women reported that they lived in fear of abuse during their current relationship.

Despite this, males can also be victims of domestic violence. A study conducted by the Canadian Center of Justice Statistics (2000) reported that 690,000 women and 549,000 men were victims of some form of spousal assault during a 5 year period in Canada, Australia, New Zealand and around the world, women are far more likely to be killed by their intimate partner than men (Rennison & Welchans, 2000).

Domestic violence is both a world wide and national crisis and has appeared at alarming threshold throughout the world. According to UNICEF Study Report (2000) 20-50 per cent of women population of the world are victims of domestic violence.

Worldwide Statistics of D.V.

The statistics of domestic violence available from various countries evince the proportion of domestic violence. The incidence rates of the various forms of domestic violence are identified in the following manner:

(1) Physical Abuse: A growing body of research studies confirm the prevalence of physical violence in all parts of the globe, including the estimates of 20-50 per cent of women from country who have sometimes or the others, experienced domestic violence. According to UNFPA world population report (2005), in every country where reliable large scale studies have been conducted, between 10 to 69 per cent of women report that they have been physically abused by an intimate

partner in their life time. Similarly in 2002, The World Health Organization surveyed many developed and developing countries and identified the prevalence rate of physical abuse of women at different levels. Figure 1.1 below presents the percent of married women ages 15-49 ever beaten* by a spouse or partner.

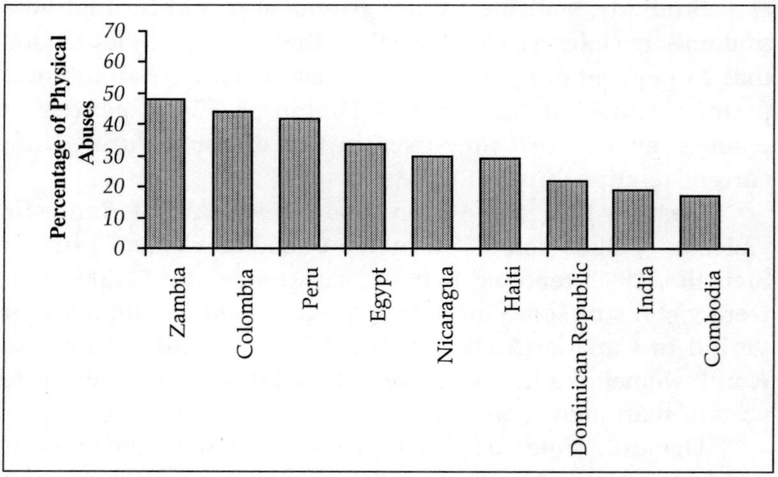

Fig. 1.1: The percent of married women aged 15-49 ever beaten by a spouse or partner

* In most surveys respondents of different countries reported having been hit, kicked, stepped, or physically hurt and abused. On prevalence rate of Physical abuse against women, Zambia stood first and India was identified at last but one place and minimum abused victims were identified in Combodia.

A numerable number of studies on violence against women indicate that;

- The perpetrators of violence against women are almost exclusively men,
- Physical abuse in intimate relationship is almost always accompanied by severe psychological and verbal abuse. In 1 of 4 cases of domestic violence, women also experienced sexual abuse.

- Women are at greater risk of violence from men they know. In Australia, Canada, Israil, South Africa and the United States, 40-70 per cent of female murder victims were killed by their partners.

Many men and women believe wife beating is justified. The shame associated with D.V., rape and other forms of abuse may contribute to the fact that women often suffer it in silence, afraid of repercussions and stigma and never tell anyone.

Table 1.1: Proportion of physically abused women who sought help from different sources, selected population based studies (WHO, 2002: World Report on Violence and Health, Geneva: WHO)

Country/Area	*Sample*	*Proportion of physically abused women who*			
		Never told%	*Contact police %*	*Told Friend %*	*Told Family%*
Australia*	6300	18	19	58	53
Bangladesh	10368	68	—	—	30
Canada	12300	22	26	45	44
Combodia	1374	34	1	33	22
Chile	1000	30	16	14	32**/ 21***
Egypt	7121	47	—	3	44
Ireland	679	—	20	50	37
Nicaragua	8507	37	17	28	34
Republic of Moldova	4790	—	6	30	31
United Kingdom	430	38	22	46	31

Source: Reproduced from reference 25 with the permission of the publisher.

* Women who are physically assaulted in past 12 months.

** Refers to the proportion of women who told their family.

*** Refers to the proportion of women who told their partner's family.

(2) Sexual Abuse: Sexual abuse and rape by husband or an intimate partner is not considered a crime in most countries and women in many societies do not consider forced sex as rape if they are married to or cohabiting with, the perpetrator. The assumption is that once a woman enters into a contract of marriage, the husband has the right to unlimited sexual access

to his wife. Relevant surveys in many countries reveal that approximately 10-15 per cent of women report being forced to have sex with their intimate partner.

Considering the taboo in most countries that surrounds the incest or the sexual abuse of females within the family, is one of the most invisible forms of violence. Because the crime is perpetrated most often by a father-in-law, husband, or another male relative in a position of trust, the rights of the female are usually sacrificed, in order to protect the name of the family and that of the adult perpetrator. However, studies have shown that from 40-60 per cent of known sexual assaults within the family are committed against girls aged 15 years and younger, regardless of region or culture. A recent study in the Netherlands shows that 45 per cent of victims of sexual violence within the domestic sphere are under the age of 18, of these, girls are far more likely to be victims of incest than boys.

Population based studies report that from 12-25 per cent of women have experienced either attempted or completed forced sex by an intimate partner or ex-partner at sometime in their lives and 38 per cent of sexually abused women were assaulted by their husbands, common law partners or boy friends (Canadian Panel on Violence Against Women, 1993).

(3) Psychological and Emotional Abuse: Since psychological violence is harder to capture in quantitative studies, a full picture of the deeper and more insidious levels of violence defies quantification. Victims survivors report that ongoing psychological violence—emotional torture and living under terror is often more unbearable than the physical brutality, with mental stress leading to a high incidence of suicide and suicide attempts. A close link between domestic violence and suicide has been established based on studies contributed in the United States, Fiji, Papua, New Guinea, Peru, India, Bangladesh and Sri Lanka. Suicide is 12 times as likely to have been attempted by a woman who has been abused than by one who has not. In United States as many as 35-40 per cent of battered women attempt suicide. In Sri Lanka, the number of suicides by girls and women in age range of 15-24 years, is 55 times greater than the number of deaths due to pregnancy and child birth.

(4) Other Forms of Abuses: Forced prostitution, foeticide or other kinds of economic abuses (commercial exploitation) by male partners or parent is another form of violence against women and children reported worldwide. Murder of women by their batterers is another phenomenon that should be regarded as a separate category when recording domestic violence. Studies carried out in Australia, Bangladesh, Canada, Kenya, Thailand and the U.S.A. have documented the incidence of homicide within the domestic sphere. In Southern Africa, women's groups have begun to document the increasing incidents of homicide and data on this issue are available from Botswana, South Africa, Switzerland, Zambia and Zimbabway. A comparative analysis of spousal homicide based on 1991 data, concluded that Russian women are 2.5 times more likely to be murdered by their partners than American women. However, American women are already twice as likely to be killed by their partners than women in Western-European countries.

Domestic violence is the most common form of gender based violence. In Northern Ghana girls are 'donated' to priests and/or forced to live as 'wives' and submit sexually to the shrine priests in return for protection of the family. A similar practice exists in Southern India, where young women and girls (Devadasi) are 'donated' to serve a temple, and very often end up being prostitute. In a Canadian study it was found that 21 per cent of women abused in an intimate relationship are abused during pregnancy. However, only 26 per cent of women abuse incidents are reported to the police (Statistics, Canada, 1993).

In a comprehensive interview with nearly 25,000 women at 15 sites in 10 countries, researchers from the World Health Organization found that rates of partner violence ranged from a low of 15 per cent in Yokohama, Japan, to a high of 71 per cent in rural Euthopia. At six of the sites, at least 50 per cent of women said that they had been subjected to moderate or severe violence in the home at some point. At 13 sites, more than a quarter of all women said that they had suffered such violence in the past year (*Times of India*, 2006; World Health Organization, 2006).

It has been published in the 'Lancet', a medical journal in London, that "violence by an intimate partner is a common experience world-wide. In all but one setting women were at far greater risk of physical or sexual violence by a partner than by other people." The report says that rural areas tend to have higher rates of abuse than cities. But no area was immune (World Health Organization Report, 2006).

While researchers and women's groups have long known that domestic violence was widespread and other smaller surveys have supported that notion, the WHO study adds an important dimension to the topic because it provides an unusual amount of quantitative, scientific data on the subject. Whereas, previous studies had focused mostly on developed countries, indeed mostly on the United States, (Claudia Garcia—Moreno, a researcher in the WHO research, 2006).

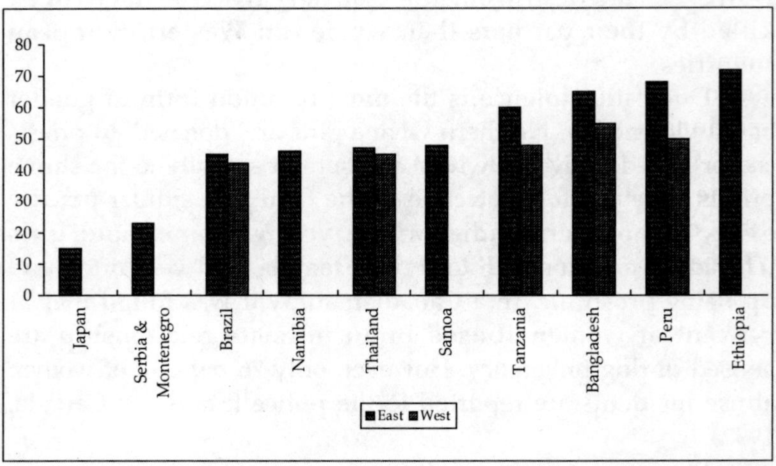

Fig. 1.2: Displays the rate of violence in various residential setting of different countries (World Health Organization Report, 2006).

The Incidence of Domestic Violence in India

Domestic violence is a worldwide phenomenon and is also epidemic in Indian society. Crime or violence against women has been recognized as one of the major social indicators in India. At the same time, there is a dearth of information on the magnitude and patterns of domestic violence in India, particularly by way of community based data. Family based data from police, court, hospital and NGO records do exist, but these data remain scattered, poorly maintained and seldom. Some studies indicate that physical abuse of Indian women is quite high ranging from 22 per cent to 60 per cent of women surveyed (Mahajan, 1990; Rao, 1996).

The National Crimes Record Bureau reveal a shocking 71.5 per cent increase in cases of torture and dowry deaths during the period from 1991 to 1995 may reflect increased reporting of violence. In 1995 torture of women constituted 29.2 per cent of all reported crimes against women. In another study 18 to 45 per cent of married man in five districts of Uttar Pradesh agreed that they physically abused their wives (Narayana, 1996). Further, in a study by Ranjana Kumari (1989) of dowry abuse, it was found that one out of every four dowry victims was driven to suicide. A frequent perception of domestic violence against women is that it is limited to physical harm perpetrated on adult women within a marital relationship.

The violence against women has been recognized as one of the critical areas of concern by Indian Government in its 1995 country report for the Fourth World Conference of Women at Beijing. The number of violent cases that are reported give just a small indication of the problem. Torture and cruelty by husband or in-laws, constituted the major kind of crime amongst all reported forms of violence against women in 1995 accounting for 29 per cent of all reported cases. Despite this, a sizable number of research studies evince the high prevalence rate of D.V. in each and every strata of society. A study on institutional responses to domestic violence was conducted by the women's studies unit at the Tata Institute of Social Sciences, Mumbai in 1997-98 to fill this gap. It was noted that the two states of Madhya Pradesh and Maharashtra together account for 29.7 per cent of total registered crimes against women. Further, Maharashtra registered the highest number of cases of torture and cruelty by husband and/or his relatives (Mitra, 2006; Pooncha, Pandey, 2006; & Visaria, 1999).

According to United Nations (UN) population fund report, as many as 70 per cent of married women in India between the age of 15-49 are victims of beating, rape or coerced sex.

According to on line survey of the Tribune (2006), two third of the women surveyed, reported some forms of psychological, physical or sexual abuses. 42 per cent experience physical beating or sexual assault, 23 per cent suffer abusive language, belittlement and threats. About 36-38 per cent of women in a Tamilnadu study and 42-48 per cent of women in Uttar Pradesh study reported violence (Jejeebhoy, 1998). In one village in Punjab 75 per cent of women from Scheduled Caste households reported regular beating (Mahajan, 1990). Once the initial inhibition was broken, it was not difficult for men to beat their wives. In most cases the problem started within the first year of marriage and before the birth of any children. Women reported that after having children, the violence did not decrease but their husbands become accustomed to abusing them. Many also felt that if they listened quietly, their husband's abuse might lie down, if instead a women defended herself or responded angrily, the confrontation usually worsened and could escalate to physical violence.

Apart from this, India has one of the highest rates of violence during pregnancy. The Washington—based International Centre for Research on Women in collaboration with independent researchers has some alarming statistics to confirm this trend. 50 per cent of women interviewed, reported to being kicked, beaten or hit when pregnant. 75 per cent of those who reported repeated violence have attempted to commit suicide.

Recently, a survey study was conducted in eastern districts of Gorakhpur by Mishra (2006). She identified a total of 268 registered cases of domestic violence ranged from physical harassments, sexual harassments to dowry deaths within the last 10 months in Gorakhpur and Basti district. However, there are more than hundred cases for which women could not ask for the judgment.

The statistics available from I.G. and D.I.G. offices of Gorakhpur and Basti Regions indicate that Gorakhpur is two step forward in violence against women as compared to Basti District. By this year (January to October, 2006) 15 cases of dowry deaths in Gorakhpur, 11 cases in Basti and maximum 22 cases in Kushinagar have been registered. The maximum cases of physical harassments have also been reported in Gorakhpur region (19) as compared to Basti region (09). If we look at the statistics of domestic violence, an increament of 10 per cent per year has been observed in registered cases, however, a numerable number of cases are unreported due to the fear of social embarrassment and threats.

Legal Efforts to Prevent Domestic Violence

The increasing rate of violence behind the closed doors, is a matter of serious concern. The cases of cruelty committed by the husband and family members are identified in plenty. However, woman concerned constitute only a small fraction of the cases involving such cruelty. Due to these reasons the Indian Penal Code viz.; the Code of Criminal Procedure, 1973 and the Evidence Act, 1972 were amended suitably to deal effectively not only with cases of dowry deaths but also cases of cruelty to married women by their husband and in-laws. However, the Vienna Accord of 1994, the Beijing Declaration and the Platform for Action, 1995 acknowledged that domestic violence is undoubtedly a human rights issue and serious deterrent in development of society. The 'United Nations Committee on Convention of Elimination of All Forms of Discrimination Against Women' (CEDAW) has recommended that State parties should act to protect women against violence of any kind, especially happening within family by husband or family members. If a woman is subjected to cruelty by her husband or his relatives, that is an offence punishable under Sec. 498-A of the Indian Penal Code. The Civil Law does not, however, address this phenomenon in its entirety, the object of protection of women from being victim of domestic violence and to prevent the occurrence of domestic violence in the society. However, the protection of women from Domestic Violence Act has been placed on 13th September, 2005.

The "Protection of Women from Domestic Violence Act" (PWDVA), 2005 (Act No. 43 of 2005): **Following objectives of the Act fully explain the reasons for the enactment of this legislation:**

1. Domestic violence is undoubtedly a human rights issue and serious deterrent to development. The Vienna Accord of 1994 and the Beijing Declaration and the Platform for Action (1995), have acknowledged this. The United Nations Committee on Convention on Elimination of All Forms of Discrimination Against Women (CEDAW) in its General Recommendation No. XII (1989) has recommended that State parties should act to protect women against violence of any kind especially that occurring within the family.

2. The incidence of domestic violence is widely prevalent but has remained largely invisible in the public domain. Presently, where a woman is subjected to cruelty by her husband or his relatives (family members), it is an offence under Sec. 498-A of the Indian Penal Code (45 of 1860). The civil law does not, however, address this phenomenon in its entirety.

3. It is, therefore, proposed to enact a law keeping in view, the rights guaranteed under Articles; 14, 15 and 21 of the Constitution to provide for a remedy under the civil law which is intended to protect the women from being victims of domestic violence and to prevent the occurrence of domestic violence in the society.

4. The Bill, *inter alia,* **seeks to provide for the following:**

(i) It covers those women who are or have been in a relationship with the abuser where both parties have lived together in a shared household and are related by consanguinity, marriage or through a relationship in the nature of marriage or adoption. In addition, relationships with family members living together as joint family are also included. Every those women who are sisters, widows, mother, single woman, or living with the abuser are entitled to get legal protection under the proposed legislation. However, where the

Bill enables the wife or the female living in a relationship in the nature of marriage to file a complaint under the proposed enactment against any relative of the husband or the male partner, it does not enable any female relative of the husband or the male partner to file a complaint against the wife or the female partner.

(ii) It defines "domestic violence" to include actual abuse or threat of abuse that is physical, sexual, verbal, emotional, or economic. Harassment by way of unlawful dowry demands to the women or her relatives would also be covered under this definition.

(iii) It provides for the rights of women to secure housing. It also provides for the right of a women to reside in her matrimonial home or shared household, whether or not she has any title or rights in such home or household. This right is secured by a residence order, which is passed by the Magistrate.

(iv) It empowers the Magistrate to pass protection orders in favour of the person (victim) to prevent the abuser from committing an act of domestic violence or any other specified act, entering a workplace or any other place frequented by the aggrieved person, attempting to communicate with her, isolating any assets used by both the parties and causing violence to the aggrieved person, her relatives or others who provide her assistance from the domestic violence.

(v) It provides for appointment of Protection Officers and registration of Non-Governmental Organisations as service providers for providing assistance to the aggrieved person with respect to her medical examination, obtaining legal aid, safe shelter, etc.

(5) The Protection of Women from Domestic Violence Act, 2005: Seeks to achieve the above objectives and include following components:

- Any harm, injury to health, safety of life, limb or well-being or any other act of threatening or coercion, etc., by any adult member of the family, constitutes domestic violence.

- Any woman who is, or has been in a domestic or family relationship, if is subjected to any act of domestic violence can complain.
- Aggrieved or affected woman can complain to the concerned protection officer, police officer, service provider or Magistrate.
- Aggrieved woman has right to be informed about the available services and free legal services, from the protection officers.
- Shelter-home and medical facilities can be provided to victimized woman.
- Interim compensation can be available to aggrieved woman.
- Proceedings of the complaint can be held in camera.
- Every aggrieved woman has right to reside in shared household.
- Protection order by Magistrate can be given in favour of aggrieved woman.
- Monetary relief can be given to aggrieved woman to meet expenses or losses.
- Appeal can be made to Sessions Court within 30 days from the order of concerned Magistrate.
- Imprisonment upto 1 year or a fine upto Rs. 20,000 or both for breach of protection order by the opposite party and;
- Protection officer can be prosecuted, up to 1 year imprisonment or with a fine upto Rs. 20,000 or both for failure of his duties.

The Protection of Women from Domestic Violence Act, 2005 (Act No. 43 of 2005), is an act to provide more effective protection of the rights of women guaranteed under the Constitution who are victims of violence of any kind occurring within the family and for matters connected therewith or incidental thereto. It extends to the whole of India except the State of Jammu and Kashmir. It has came into force on

26th October, 2005. The Power, authority and responsibilities of Government officials viz., Protection Officers, Police Officers, Service Providers and Magistrate have been well defined under this act and aggrieved (victim) will be given immediate relief or help as soon as the complaint of D.V. is received by helping agencies i.e. Police, Court etc. (for details, see Bare Act, PWDVA, 2005).

Any person who has reason to believe that an act of domestic violence has been, or is being, or is likely to be committed, may give information about it to the concerned Protection Officer. A Police Officer, Protection Officer, Service Provider or Magistrate who has received a complaint of domestic violence or is otherwise present at the place of an incident of domestic violence or when the incident of domestic violence is reported to him, shall inform the aggrieved person:

(a) of her right to make an application for obtaining a relief by way of a protection order, an order for monetary relief, a custody order, a residence order, a compensation order or more than one such order;
(b) of the availability of services of service providers;
(c) of the availability of services of the protection officers;
(d) of her right to free legal services under the Legal Services Authorities Act, 1987 (39 of 1987);
(e) of her right to file a complaint under Sec.498-A, of the Indian Penal Code, (45 of 1860) wherever relevant.

Duties of shelter homes or medical facilities is that if an aggrieved person or on her behalf a protection officer or a service provider requests the person in charge of a shelter home or medical facility to provide shelter or medical aid to her, such person in-charge of the shelter home or medical facility shall provide shelter or medical aid to the aggrieved person.

The Magistrate may, after giving the aggrieved person (victim) and the respondent (perpetrator) an opportunity of being heard and on being *prima facie* satisfied that DV has taken place or is likely to take place, pass a protection order in favour of the aggrieved person and prohibit the respondent from committing any act of domestic violence. While disposing of an application under sub-section of Sec. 12, the Magistrate may direct the respondent to pay monetary relief to meet the expenses incurred and losses suffered by the aggrieved person and any child of the aggrieved person as a result of the Domestic Violence (DV).

The Magistrate may, at any stage of hearing of the application for protection order or for any other relief grant temporary custody of any child or children to the aggrieved person or the person making an application on her behalf and specify, if necessary, the arrangements for visit of such child or children by the respondent. The Magistrate may, on an application being made by the aggrieved person, pass an order directing the respondent to pay compensation and damages for the injuries, including mental torture and emotional distress, caused by the acts of DV committed by that respondent (Perpetrator).

Contributing Factors of Domestic Violence

Since Domestic Violence (DV) is a major psycho-social problem and its causative roots are multifaceted; this problem can not be understood on the basis of a single factor. Current approaches to analyze the D.V. emphasize an interlinked cluster of individual, family, environmental and socio-cultural risk factors that can result in increased risk of abuses. Multiple forces determine it at multiple levels; the individual (ontogenetic factors), the family (the micro-system) level, the community (the exo-system) and the cultural (the macro system) level in which all the factors are nested to each other. Table 1.2 displays a frame work of the causative factors of Domestic Violence (DV) which is based on Belsky's (1984) theory of the maltreatment.

This framework includes psychological disturbances in perpetrator, (abusive husband) eliciting characteristics of wife/ children, dysfunctional patterns of family interaction, stress-inducing social forces, and abuse promoting cultural values. The model is mainly based on Bronferbrenner's (1977, 1979) work related to the ecology of human development which conceptualized maltreatment as a "Social-Psychological Phenomenon" and multiple forces determine it. Belsky combined Tinbergen's concern for ontogenetic development with Bronferbrenner's concern for the ecology (or the context) for developing his conceptual model of maltreatment. He assumed that forces within the individual determine maltreatment; the family, the culture and these determinants are nested ecologically with one another.

Table 1.2: The Causes of Domestic Violence

Ontogenetic Factors	*Micro -System Factors*	*Exo-System Factors*	*Macro-System Factors*
History of abuse	Marital Discord, Conflict	Inadequate health care facilities	Economic recession
Alcohol abuse	Single parent-hood	Soial isolation	Cultural accep-tance of corporal punishment
Stressful experiences	Premature or unhealthy child	Unsafe neigh-bourhood	View of females/ children as possessions
Low I.Q. Psychiatric and Physical illness	—	—	Patriarchy

Thus, causes of maltreatment cannot be explained on the basis of a single factor. It is the product of multiple factors interlocked with each other. Despite the personal characteristics, several interaction variables at the level of family, community, society and culture play prominent role. Thus, in order to understand the gravity of domestic violence, it is essential to focus on social as well as psychological aspects of the violence behind the closed doors.

(i) Social Factors of Domestic Violence

Numerous social/contextual factors play prominent role in the root of domestic violence. Therefore, some of the major social factors have been discussed in this section.

Patriarchy and Power Hierarchy

In Indian families, the man enjoys absolute authority, power and privileges and makes every decision as the undisputed "head of family." He is addressed and elevated to the position of the "annadata (giver of grains) and "Grihkarta" (household authority). The well-known 19th century social reformer from Bengal, 'Raja Ram Mohan Roy' remarked, "At marriage, the wife is recognized as half of her husband, but in conduct they are treated worse than inferior animals." Roy's sympathetic observation was a reaction to the prevalent social attitudes of the time which was demeaning to women. To control women at every stage of their existence is an accepted act of manliness (Karlekar, 1998).

An analysis of the power hierarchy within the conjugal home would suggest some identifiable features—a gendered division of labour, the fact that in most Indian marriages women enter as strangers into an already structured world, the creation of a permanent inequality in the relationship of the natal and conjugal homes, and overarching domestic ideologies that legislate gender status and role. Like other theorists of the family, Karlekar also makes a significant distinction between "family" and "household". The household is a physical structure, localized, and a specific constellation of emotional and economic relationships among its core members. The family is more amorphous, seen as larger kinship groupings, spread over time and space. The household, then, is "the operational unit" that provides the ground, so to speak, for a working out of family ideologies around specific roles and expectations. Further, "inequality is embedded in oppressive structures of a family ideology committed to an age and gender hierarchy which is worked out within a household" (Karlekar, 1998).

Most field studies on domestic violence reveal that women, having internalized patriarchal norms, often do not perceive themselves as abused unless they have suffered severe physical assault. Many women continue to endure violence even while recognizing its criminality because of the absence of support structures in the community at large.

The concept of ownership, in turn legitimizes control over women's gender which in many law codes has been deemed essential to ensure patrilineal inheritance. Violence was an important indicator of women's autonomy and power within the household.

Any traditional custom that places women in subordinate positions within society or in the family has the potential to turn violent. The putative sacredness of a traditional marriage, rigid ideas of conjugality, and patriarchal traditions of family structure take precedence over concerns for women or children. It has been observed that whenever male authority is threatened, the lives of women and children become redundant, and are considered dispensable. This differential access to power and resources would lead to a redivision of household labour among women, relationships of antagonism between them, and a re-entrenching of patriarchy as the more privileged of the female members function as the surrogate (and, often, violent) agents of male hegemony and control. While women's collectivity remains a cherished feminist ideal, the very nature of the traditional family discourages such an aligning. This is why most abused women articulate the feeling of isolation even in non nuclear families where there are other women members.

Family Structure

Family structure is associated with the probability of domestic violence. In a study of domestic violence in the Indian context, Karlekar (1998) identified certain generic characteristics of the family and the "naturalization" of violence within it (Karlekar, 1998). Whether the basic family unit is joint or nuclear, it provides the ground for both power play and powerlessness along the lines of gender and age. Violence—understood not only as physical harm but also as discrimination, deprivation, denial of access to resources, intimidation, exploitation, and other means, whereby economic and social inequality is perpetuated—is the tool that reproduces the inherently hierarchical structure of the family (Ghosh, 2004). Those most vulnerable to familial violence are women and children. Moreover in 30 per cent to 60 per cent of families where either child and wife battering or child maltreatment is occurring, one will find that the other forms of violence are also being perpetrated (Edleson, 1999). In the second nation wide survey of domestic violence, Straus and Gelles (1990) found that men who reported beating their wives were also more likely to report abusing their children.

Socio-Economic Status

The incidence of domestic violence is found at higher rate in poor, disadvantaged and low strata of society. Family of low S.E.S. is felt high not only on rates of violence but also growing up with poverty has a substantial effect on the well-being of females and children (Brooks-Gunn & Duncan, 1997; Schteingart *et al.,* 1995). Poverty has a significant, yet, indirect effect on female's adjustment, most likely because of its association with such negative influences, particularly harassment and elevated exposure to acute and chronic stressor that define the day to day experiences of women in poverty (McLoyd, 1998). It has been observed that woman from the upper and middle classes are unprepared for the trauma associated with domestic violence. As a result, they suffer from a sense of isolation and shame, and for years try and conceal the fact that their husbands are abusive. However, women from all classes are discouraged to leave abusive marriage.

Social Isolation

Social isolation of the family is one of the commonly noted features of abusive families, coupled with stressful living conditions, such as lack of adequate day care, peer groups or close friends, and adequate housing (Garbarino, 1976). Social isolation, however, is not a single factor but, rather a set of variables linked to the family's perception of support and their networks (Coohey, 1996; Thompson, 1994).

Social Structure, Religion, Caste and Community

A sizable number of research findings (Mitra, 2006; Poonacha & Pandey, 2006; & Visaria, 1999) evince that domestic violence is witnessed across all religion, caste and education lines, the most widespread violence was reported among the women from the Thakone and Baraiya castes (80%) other low caste (75%) and Scheduled Caste (74%). Though relatively less, large numbers of Muslim women (56%) and high caste of women (45%) also reported abuse from their husbands. Differences in the rates of physical abuse account for most of the variation between caste groups while all women reported similar rates of psychological abuse (23% to 28%), a smaller proportion of high caste women (17%) additionally reported physical abuse compared to low caste women (57%).

Reported violence declined with the increasing education of both men or women. Abusive relationships were reported more frequently among illiterate women (76%) and illiterate men (81%) than women and men with secondary schooling or more (42% and 53%). Violence also varied with living arrangements. 53 per cent of women in joint families reported abuse compared to 73 per cent of women in nuclear families. It is to note that rate of psychological violence among both groups is the same. The 20 per cent difference is due to higher numbers of women in nuclear families reporting physical abuse.

When grouped by age and duration of marriage, all category of women reported either psychological or physical abuse at incidence levels ranging from 60 per cent to 70 per cent.

The data suggest that as women have been married longer, forms of violence actually shift towards more physical violence, while women who had been married 1 to 5 years reported similar levels of physical and psychological violence (35% and 40%). The responses of women who had been married 11-15 years demonstrated a shift towards more physical violence, about 51 per cent of these women reported physical abuse and 18 per cent reported psychological abuse (Visaria, 1999).

Around the world, women and girls suffer from the harmful and life threatening effects of traditional and cultural practices that continue under the guise of cultural and social evolutions and religious beliefs. There is no single factor to account for violence perpetrated against them.

Cultural Factors

Cultural ideologies both in industrialized and developing countries provide 'legitimacy' for violence against women in certain circumstances. Religious and historical traditions in the past have sanctioned the chastising and beating of wives. The physical punishment of wives has been particularly sanctioned under the notion of entitlement and ownership of women. Main control of family wealth inevitably places decision-making authority into male hands, leading to male dominance and proprietary rights over women and girls.

Thus, along with the burden of child care and the sexual stereotyping of parental responsibility force women to remain in violent homes. Under the circumstances, a man does not need to fear that if he abuses (beats) his wife, she will leave him with the responsibility of looking after the children. So he can continue abusing his wife with relative impurity. He can be relatively confident that she will not leave him because, (a) she is not economically independent, (b) she has no place to go and (c) she has the responsibility of child rearing because society feels that child care is exclusively a mother's job and women who leave the children behind become ridiculed and social out castes.

Review of studies thus, evinces the detrimental role of numerous social factors in the origin and prevalence of domestic violence. Thus, certain social/contextual factors were selected for present investigation.

Despite this, to understand the process of domestic violence, the role of psychological variables should be examined.

(ii) Psychological Factors of Domestic Violence

Although, earlier 1960's studies confirmed that domestic violence is rooted in adult's psychological disturbances and abusive people (perpetrators) were identified as abused victim in their own childhood (Kempe *et al.*, 1962). However, later studies evinced the role of multiple causative factors, embedded with each other in the root of violence behind closed doors (Flavia, 1988; Pandey & Mishra, 2000; & Straus *et al.* 1980).

In a classical study, Flavia (1988) surveyed a huge amount of cases suffering from acute physical violence. She analyzed the role of socio-psychological factors in the prevalence of D.V. in our society. The researcher pointed out that after marriage the woman becomes the property of husband. The definition of the rape law says 'forced intercourse with a woman other than his wife.' This statement implies that a husband can rape his own wife or have intercourse without her consent. Even though society does not actually say that a man has the right to beat his wife, no one denies that he has the right to tame the woman he marries, or make her low to his will. So, when a man cannot tame his wife in any other way he uses force. Consequently, the incidence of D.V. is witnessed at an epidemic proportion in our society and no society, class, community is free from this epidemic.

Aggression and violence are considered to be positive male qualities. The man who is not assertive in his marriage becomes an object of ridicule. He is called 'henpecked.' Women themselves accept the subordinate role within marriage unquestioningly. Society either pretends that wife beating does not exist or treats it as a very light matter. This attitude leads to the persistence of D.V. in our society. There are certain myths associated with domestic violence.

(1) The first myth about D.V. is that middle class women do not suffer physical abuses. Reports reveal that women from all sections of the society, belonging to different religions, and all educational levels and from all socio-economic classes suffer physical or psychological abuses. The middle and upper class women are abused behind closed doors. They live in total isolation. Psychological impact of physical abuse is less in working class women. This could also be

because employed women do not see it as being something related to them as individuals.

(2) Another myth regarding D.V. is that the victim of violence is a small fragile, helpless woman not belonging to the working class. But in fact, women holding responsible jobs as doctors, lecturers, journalist and models also get also physical assault by their husbands.

(3) Similarly, not only D.V. is committed by men who belong to lower strata of society or a man who is unemployed or frustrated in his job, an alcoholic, or a mentally sick person, aggressive in his relationship with the world at large but also the professionals like lawyers and doctors are also beating their wives. 60 per cent of the middle class women who were interviewed said that their husbands did not touch alcohol. Among the rest only 20 per cent of the men beat their wives after the consumption of alcohol. Among the working class although 80 per cent of the men consumed alcohol, in most cases they beat their wives while they were sober and wanted money to buy their drink (Flavia, 1988).

(4) Another myth identified about D.V. is that of provocation. This myth victimizes the woman further. The burden of guilt falls on the woman and increases her shame and degradation. This myth also conveys the message that women who get beaten are masochistic and they want to get beaten.

(5) Another myth is that long standing battering relationships can change for the better. With the passage of time the violent assaults are reduced in severity and frequency. But the women continue to live in a state of fear and uncertainty because they can never predict when, where and under what circumstances the violence may suddenly be committed again. And many times the violent situation escalates into homicide and suicide.

(6) Likewise, the myth that the loving husband does not indulge in wife beating is also false. Husband can be

extremely kind and loving especially after a violent assault.

(7) Another myth is that since the women don't leave their husbands they do not mind the physical assaults (abuses) or that they actually like it. It is often asked: 'Why do women continue to live in a situation where they are eventually murdered or are driven to suicide? Why don't they seek a way out? The theory of learned helplessness (Seligman, *et al.* 1975) gives an insight into the mental state of passive resignation experienced by these women.

Domestic Violence: Perspective of the Learned Helplessness

Most women (abused victim) interviewed, attempted to break away from their husbands during the first year of their marriage. They often went to stay with their mothers. But in most cases the women were told that it would not happen again; that she should have a child.

When the middle class women were beaten for the first time they were numb with shock. Every woman interviewed said 'I did not know that educated men assault their wives.' They had not seen wife beating or D.V. in their parents' home. Their initial reaction was to deny it even to themselves. They said the shame and humiliation of the first beating had left a permanent scar on their psyche. They became silent and withdrawn. They did not tell anyone. This reluctance to confide ranged from a few weeks to five years. After the initial shock they began to question their worth. They began to wonder whether there was something wrong with their behaviour, their upbringing or their education. They tried to change their behaviour, their actions and their mode of dressing in order to please the husband and in-laws. But soon they began to realize the fact that they were beaten, no matter what their reactions were. The repeated assaults threatened their physical safety and survival became a major issue.

It is at this stage women seek help. But wherever, they go they are sent back without getting any solution. The women who come back get totally disillusioned. Most return on the husband's terms. Life becomes a mere existence, often for the sake of the children. Family and friends rejoice because the couple is reunited or because the woman has learnt to adjust. In this survey it was found that the beatings continued. But the women had learnt to accept the violence as something inevitable, a fact to live with and die with. But years later the women begin to think of leaving the house once again, this time when they feel that the lives of their children were being threatened. Thus, it was noticed that women leave their home either during the first five years or when the children are grown up.

Despite societal conditioning women no longer said marriage is the ultimate goal of a woman and choose not to remain beaten. They had no hesitation to break the 'sacred knot of marriage'. But it is only when they realized that there is no way out, that they were trapped within the marriage because of—(a) lack of education, (b) economic dependency, (c) lack of support structures, (d) the difficulties in obtaining divorce/job/ house, (e) the burden of child care, that they became passive, resigned and negative in their approach. They had numbed themselves. They are abused by husband and the negative response of society to their needs had succeeded in making the women helpless, passive and negative.

The Cycle Theory of Violence

The researcher (Flavia, 1988) interpreted her findings on the basis of cycle theory of violence. In her study most women had similar stories to recall. The husbands were very considerate after a beating. After sometime the tension begins to mount, small fights leading to a big bang and then the calm, loving husband.

These experiences support Walker's (1979) three-phase theory of wife battering, (1) a tension building period followed by, (2) acute battering and, (3) then the calm-loving respite. The women who have gone through many such cycles know the pattern well. These women—the ones who are put out of their houses, hospitalized or seek the aid of institutions are the ones who are further victimized. The woman leaves the house when the man is in phase. The social workers and counselors find it very difficult to accept the women's version of the battering.

There is yet one more trend among the modern social workers and psychotherapists. They accept the fact that the man is at fault. But they attribute this fact to the man's mental condition. They tell the woman that he is a sick man and that he needs help. The woman is given the responsibility of case. The message implied is that only she can give the psychological and social help that he needs. If she leaves him, he will fall apart. She is his only hope as he refuses to seek help outside.

Thus, the women are physically and psychologically abused by their husbands and family members and then kept in their place by a society that is indifferent to their plight. They are blamed for getting beaten and then blamed for not ending their beatings. In this way, they lack social support. Women are blamed for not seeking help, yet when they do so, they are advised to go home and stop their own inappropriate behaviour. Not only are they held responsible for their own beatings, they must also assume responsibility for their husbands' mental health. Sometimes they are suggested to tolerate and find their own way to check victimization.

Before the woman realizes, the calm, loving behaviour gives way to a few batterings and verbal abuse and the cycle begins once again. When the cycle is repeated many times, the women's suppressed rage leads to loss of control, and some times women stab or last lack with lethal weapons causing serious injury. The men do not seem to benefit in any way by their violent behaviour. While trying to possess the woman psychologically, and physically dominating them, in actual fact they lose the love and respect of the woman. They may gain their fear and obedience. But the wives resent the husband's because they do not possess this power. The resentment builds up into anger and the woman tries to retaliate in other ways—sexual deprivation or verbal assault—which further deteriorates the situation and the various forms of abuses start, continue, sustain and sometimes lead to very violent and serious consequences.

Apart from the findings of Flavia study, a sizable number of studies on domestic violence evinces that psychological dynamics of domestic violence involves multiple factors including developmental, cognitive, motivational and affective processes, nested with each other. In this section, the role of certain psychological factors in the origin of domestic violence has been discussed.

Developmental Factors in Domestic Violence

(i) Socialization: Female socialization has been viewed as an important causal factor leading to domestic violence against women. Kishwar (1994) has rightly pointed out that when a girl is married and sent to her husband's family, her parents and family members say, "We are sending your 'Doli' today may only your Arthi (Ashes) emerge from that house (husband's house)". Kishwar's remark can be appreciated if it is understood that the real killer of women is gender based socialization and imposition of ill customs on girls who are maltreated behind closed doors (Pandey & Mishra, 2000) in the forms of infanticides, homicides, mental torture, sexual harassment etc.

The socialization process emphasizes on modesty and adaptation for females, while it teaches male children to be aggressive, assertive, superior and independent (Baig, 1976; De-Sauza, 1975; Jain, 1975; & Nanda, 1976). The different qualities of males and females are reinforced from childhood by all socializing agents guided by traditional concepts of proper feminine behaviour and aware that their actions are inextricably linked to family honour, prestige and ultimately material rewards, women typically carry out their roles as obedient daughters and dutiful wives (Jacobson, 1977).

The status of a wife improves upon the birth of children (particularly a male baby). As a mother of son, she is given higher 'esteem in the family', a greater degree of independence and the right to have her voice heard in the women's quarters (Mandelbaum, 1949).

(ii) Sex Stereotypes: Sex role stereotypes are the rigid fixed ideas of what is appropriate to masculine and feminine behaviour. They imply a belief that "masculine" and "feminine" are two distinct and mutually exclusive categories and that an individual's behaviour must be one or the other. These ideas pervade nearly every culture. In a society the two sexes (male and female) have been stereotyped in terms of different tasks, privileges and role patterns that are traditionally assigned to them. Children are put under strong social pressure to conform to these sex-role stereotypes, regardless of their natural dispositions. During the process of socialization boys and girls are reared differently. Boys are encouraged and reinforced to develop masculine characteristics (aggression, dominance, independence, sense of adventure, high risk taking behaviour and achievement oriented outlook) whereas, girls are encouraged to acquire feminine characteristics i.e. submissiveness, nurturance, dependence, low achievement orientation. The existence of sex stereotypes has been sufficiently documented from studies on children (Williams & Best, 1982), college students (Bem,1974; Spence & Helmreich, 1978) and women (Rao & Rao, 1982; Ward and Sethi, 1983). Researches thus, suggest that sex stereotype is an universal phenomenon and has link with gender inequality and domestic violence.

(iii) Gender Inequality and Value of Son: In traditional Indian society the role of women as a wife or as a mother are clearly defined and separated from that of husband and father. Women are considered inferior and less desirable. Therefore, male children are highly valued than female children, and they are socialized in different manner. Female children are still considered as economic liability to the parents and family (Pandey, 2001)

Because of the importance accorded to a son who is believed to save the father from going to hell, the position of a mother with sons improves more. Mother-son relations are described as strong, close, affectionate, dependable and tender. Son is highly valued because of multiple socio-economic, religious and cultural factors whereas; girls are treated less desirable due to economic burden (dowry arrangements) liabilities and many socio-cultural factors.

(iv) Women's Life Style and Domestic Violence: Certain expectations are attributed to the life style of women in Indian society, for example, it is expected that if a girl is married and has some children, she should remain happy for the rest of her life. But such expectations become false when a number of psychological problems arise out of domestic violence. Apart from the number of such problems related with the rules of marriage or unemployed life partner, there are other problems such as discrimination and attitude towards females, false, cognitions, and attribution biases towards domestic violence practices. The seriousness of such problems can be imagined by looking at the statistics available for abused victims. This trend helps to interpret the incidences of domestic violence and crimes in all strata of society. (Ghadially, 1988; Susan, 1988)

Cognitive and Attitudinal Processes in Domestic Violence

Women and children have been victimized by male aggression, particularly sexual aggression, across recorded history. During the last few decades researchers have taken interest to study this phenomenon systematically. The women's movement has been a primary impetus in stimulating scientific attention (Brown & Ziefert, 1988; Ghadially, 1988). Earlier studies and services focused mostly on victims, assessing public and professional attitudes toward victims, developing treatment services and establishing incidence and prevalence rates. Various forms of domestic violence against women *i.e.,* wife battering, sexual assault and psychological abuses have common roots in patriarchal values and practices in our society.

Researchers reported marked differences in the various types of violence against women. These differences centered on the relative frequencies of preventive interventions and attitudinal studies. Brown and Ziefert (1988) reviewed a numerable number of studies and report and there were three intervention studies to prevent battering, none to prevent sexual harassments or rape. On the other hand, while there were no studies found on attitude towards battered victims, there were four on attitude towards abused victims and one on attitude towards perpetrators (rapists).

Some studies surveyed attitudes about rape abused victims and their attackers. A common finding in this research is significant gender difference in the degree of blame imposed on the victims. Men more than women participants, believe that the women who was attacked, to be responsible in varying degrees for being harassed. This difference was particularly striking in surveys of predominantly male physicians and all females' crisis counselors (King, Rotter, Calhoun & Selby, 1978) and mental health professionals (Resick & Jackson, 1981).

The seriousness of domestic violence issues and status of women in India and all over the world can be imagined on the basis of considerable attention paid by social scientists, psychologists, government organizations, women organizations and social support groups. The reports submitted by these groups have considered domestic violence as the most pervasive factor in the low status of women in India. Apart from this, men have always been taught to perceive themselves as superior to women. This training makes them believe that they have to control their wives, especially if they are considered disobedient. This perspective of superiority, orient them to commit cruelty against their wives.

The earliest article on women battering or domestic violence raises serious questions about the attitudes of researchers themselves in studying this issue. Kahn and Behavioural Health Technician Staff (1980) examined socio-cultural variables and their impact on wife beating in an aboriginal community in Northern Australia. They found that wife and girlfriend beating were a routine occurrence in the community supported by cultural norms that stemmed from a view of women as men's property. They also found that the beating were interpreted by some as expressions of caring, they concluded that the practice cannot be totally condemned since it would negate an important aspect of the community's culture.

A critical factor in evaluating this work is an understanding of the context of domestic violence. Women are physically abused most often by their husbands. Although the history of domestic violence in the form of women battering and sexual harassments incorporates patriarchal attitudes and beliefs about women as men's property, there is a wide range of consciousness of gender issues in the review work of 27 articles organized into four broad themes: Attitude towards victims and perpetrators, ways women are affected by and cope with domestic violence services and educational facilities to abused victims.

Coping with Domestic Violence

A study by Riger, Gordon and Bailly (1982) evinces a high level of awareness of the historical context of violence against women. They looked at the ways women's usages of protective behaviour are affected by neighbourhood conditions, psychological factors and life circumstances. Earlier research has shown that self protecting behaviours can include avoidance which reduces exposure to risk, and risk management which includes measures taken to deal with risk when the person cannot avoid it. Fear explained the largest proportion of avoidance behaviours. Researchers argue how protective behaviours interact with sex role prescription by continuing to encourage dependence and by limiting women's access to resources.

Based on the survey of battered women, Mitchell and Hodson (1983) concluded that women with greater personal resources made more supporting responses from informal and formal sources of help and less avoidant coping styles are more likely to show less deleterious effects. Women who had been exposed to family violence to childhood were found to use more avoidant and less active coping responses than men, to have access to fewer resources, to feel pessimistic about their friends' abilities or willingness to help and to have less supportive networks (Rosenberg, *et al.,* 1985). In a study of difference in problem solving skill of battered and non battered rural women, Claerhout, Elder and Janes (1982) found that the non battered women generated more alternatives when faced with violent situation. Battered women produced more avoidant and dependent responses and did not typically perceived alternative ways of behaving. Researchers noted the need to provide women at risk with problem solving skill training.

A close perusal of review of studies reveals the significance of investigating domestic violence in relation to interact ional, affective and cognitive processes. Therefore, marital conflict, life stress and empowerment were selected as psychological variables for present research study. These variables are discussed in the following section.

(1) Marital Conflict

Marital conflict is one of the most important determinants of domestic violence. It is well established that people who are stressed in other areas of their life also report being unhappily married. For example, marital satisfaction has been found to covary with a diverse range of negative life stressors and states, such as the quality of life, job stress, a variety of dysfunctional personality characteristics, and depression (Barton & Dreger, 1986, Beach, Arias & O. Leary, 1986; Burgess, Locke & Thomes, 1971; Krokoff, 1984; Lewark, Wakefield & Briggs, 1985; Smolen, Spiegel & Martin, 1986; Yogev, 1986). Straus *et al.* (1980) identified that marital conflict and violence are often associated with domestic violence. They estimated that approximately 40 per cent of the families where the adults were violent towards each other; there was also violence towards a child at some point during a 12 month period. Investigators reported that in fact marital conflicts and violence most often arise during disagreements over household responsibilities i.e.; child rearing, discipline and each partner's responsibility in child care (Hilton, 1992; Edleson, Eisikovits, Guttmann & Sela-Amit, 1991). Tragically, marital violence and family turmoil not only frighten and disturb children in a direct manner, but the resulting fallout from such events-ranging from changes in financial status, loss of family unity and safety-prolongs the stress and harmful impact on family and children. Happily married couples have been found to display higher ratios of agreement to disagreement (Gottman, 1979) and exhibit more positive nonverbal cues (Birchler, 1977; Haynes, Follingslad & Sullivan, 1979), more agreement and approval (Vincent & Friedman, 1979), and less coercive and attacking behaviours (Billings, 1979) than unhappily married couples.

Self-report measures of marital satisfaction may, in part, reflect a general stress dimension rather than something specific about the marriage. An assessment of marital quality that is independent of couple's own ratings would add precision to understanding the relationship between functioning in the marital and child systems. Such an assessment is possible using the quantitative observation of marital interaction (Gottman, 1979; Weiss & Summers, 1983).

Observing couples discussing issues important to their relationship is now an established approach for specifying dimensions of marital quality (Markman & Notarins, 1987). In one of the earliest studies of marriage, Terman, Butterweiser, Ferguson, Johnson and Wilson (1938) reported that husband's marital grievances were most likely to involve their wives' complaining, criticizing, and escalating emotion, whereas wives' grievances were most likely to involve their husbands' emotional withdrawal. Gottman (1993) reported that marriages headed toward dissolution are characterized by contempt, particularly by the wife. When spouses are contemptuous towards each other, they communicate a sense of superiority and moralistic disapproval through insults, mockery, or attributions of the partner's incompetence. Contemptuous statements are often accompanied by belligerent demands in which the spouse contests his or her partner's statements by trying to provoke a response or get a rise out of the partner.

Research on marriage has consistently demonstrated that the way couples resolve conflict is important in differentiating between happily and unhappily married couples (Gottman, 1979; Olson, Spengle & Russell, 1979; Raush, Barry, Hertel & Swam, 1974; Vincent, Weiss & Birchler, 1975). Happily married couples have been found to display higher ratios of agreement to disagreement (Gottman, 1979) and exhibit more positive nonverbal cues (Birchler, 1977; Haynes, Follingslad & Sullivan, 1979), more agreement and approval (Vincent & Friedman, 1979) and less coercive and attacking behaviours (Billings, 1979) than unhappily married couples.

One of the most consistent discriminator between happily and unhappily married couples has been the degree of negative affect expressed during conflict resolution, unhappily married couples have been found to show more negative affect reciprocity than happily married couples (Gottman, 1979). The specific conflict resolution strategies that couples use to resolve marital disagreements appear to predict internalizing and externalizing behaviour patterns.

(2) Life Stress and Domestic Violence

The adverse consequences of stress on females have been documented in a number of studies (Cartwright,1993; Pandey & Srivastava, 2004). Such consequences include emotional problems, mental illness, physical illness and social deviance. Stressful conditions are assumed either to have a direct effect on these consequences or to moderate the relationship between other factors and their consequences.

These consequences cannot be attributed to a single stressful condition, but are the result of complex processes in which stressor plays a more or less important role.

Concept of Stress

Stress is a dynamic condition in which an individual is confronted with an opportunity, constraint or demand related to what he or she desires and for which the outcome is perceived to be both uncertain and important Psychologists have endeavoured to define 'stress' and some of the representative definitions are given below:

Selye (1956) has defined stress as the nonspecific response to any demand. Selye's concept of 'General Adaptation Syndrome (GAS)' describes the stress, when an individual is confronted with a threat the general physiological response is produced in three stages i.e., alarm stage, resistance stage and exhaustion stage. Whereas Lazarus (1966) stated that stress exists, when the demands of a person are perceived as taxing or exceeding than person's adjustive capacity.

Ruff and Korchin (1967) defined stress as strenuous effort to maintain essential function at required level. Wolman (1973) defines stress as a condition of physical or mental strain, which produces changes in the automatic nervous system whereas, Cox and Cooper (1988) has defined stress as "perceptual phenomenon arising from a comparison between the demand on the person and his ability to cope. An imbalance on this mechanism while coping is important, gives rise to the experience of stress and to stress responses."

Based upon these definitions and others, stress is defined as a perceived dynamic state involving uncertainty about something important. The dynamic state can be associated with opportunities, constraints or demands.

State of opportunity are perceived by the individual to offer the potential fulfilment of important needs and values. States of constraint are perceived to be blocking or preventing current fulfilment of important needs and values. States of demands are those of the physical environment such as noise, heat and toxic chemicals which influence important needs and values both perceptually as well objectively (Schuler, 1980).

On the basis of various definitions an effort has been made to analyze why appraisal of stressful events exercise negative impact on biological, cognitive, emotional and behavioural functioning of persons.

1. The Response Based Approach: Selye (1950-1956) viewed stress as the non-specific (physiological) response of the body to any demand made upon it. He viewd stress as the response of organism to the demands of his environment. This model describes that when an organism is confronted with a threat, the general physiological response is produced in three stages i.e. alarm stage, resistance stage and exhaustion stage. However, McGrath (1970) pointed out several limitations of response based definition of stress. It fails to allow the identification of stressors prospectively and may lead to

diffused understanding, as the same response can be implied as an indicator of stress in the case of one stimulus and unrelated to stress in connection with other.

2. The Stimulus Based Approach: In this approach, stress is considered as independent variable, as an objective property of the external environment. In this sense stress is viewed in terms of the stimulus characteristics of environments which are recognized as disturbing in some form. Welford (1973) suggests that stress arises whenever there is a departure from optimum conditions which the person is unable, or not easily able to correct. Cox (1988) pointed out that stress does not exist infront of the eyes of subject or the experimenter.

The stimulus and response approaches are circular and taken separately, cannot properly explain the nature of stress. According to Lazarus and Folkman (1984), "a stimulus is stressor where it produces a stressful (psychological/ behavioural) response and a response is stressful when it is produced by a demand, threat, harm or loss".

3. Transactional Model of Stress: Some psychologists (Cox & Mackay, 1978) have proposed that stress is an individual phenomenon ; it can be best explained as a complex and a dynamic system of interaction between person and environment. The transactional approach views stress as a multi causal system. Lazarus and Folkman (1984) identify stress as a "particular relationship between the person and environment, which is appraised by the person as taxing or exceeding his or her resources and endangering the well-being." The person-environment relationship is mediated by two critical processes, i.e. cognitive appraisal and coping. If normal coping is ineffective, stress is prolonged and abnormal responses may occur.

Psychologists have shown meager interest in studying stress in India, for a long period (Krishnan, 1972). Their main focus of interest was on examining the incidence of different types of mental health problems and their demographic and social correlates.

Asthana (1985) has also made an effort to analyze the phenomenon of stress. After reviewing the stimulus—response and psychodynamic approaches, he has presented an outline of phenomenological perspective on stress. He focuses attention to the feeling of stress experience and suggests to use phenomenological analysis of the phenomenon of stress.

The variation in conceptualization of stress is largely due to confining stress to either stimulus situation or treating it as an environmental input independent of the reaction or the state of mind of the person. It is now, generally, felt that such an assumption is fraught with many limitations and appraisal of the relationship between demands on the person and his or her capabilities to meet them is very crucial. The view is supported by Lazarus *et al.*, who treats stress as a relational, experiential and cognitive phenomenon. Within this framework, stress is considered as "a relationship between the person and the environment that is appraised by the person as taxing or exceeding his or her resources and endangering his or her well-being" (Folkman, 1984).

Stress—Abuse Relationship

In recent years, researchers are showing interest to the studies of stress in family environment (Pestonjee, 1992). Investigators interested in clarifying the nature of stress and its relationship to family conflict, domestic violence or child development have evinced that a single stressor, such as sudden financial pressures, that may have triggered an abusive episode is not typically sufficient to account for the development of maladaptive behaviour among abused victims. In most cases, stress can best be described as a disequilibrating event that temporarily disturbs the functioning of family member(s) and initiates a chain of adaptive or maladaptive responses (Rutter, 1983). Similarly, assuming that domestic violence/child abuse is a form of stress that is linearly connected to certain negative outcomes warrants caution. The impact of stress is not uniform and seldom predictable, because it depends on factors such as the age, prior interactions with perpetrator and his/her interpretation of acts.

The above clarification of what constitutes stress has important implications for conceptualizing the relationship between uncontrollable events and family conflict. Rather than having a direct influence, the presence of stressful stimuli may affect the "timing" or contingent relationship between husband and wife. For example, women who were repeatedly subjected to high rates of adverse events (e.g., conflict with family members or relatives, etc.) were more inconsistent in matching their disciplinary actions to the behaviour of their children than women living in less stressful circumstances (Dumas & Walker, 1985).

Researchers have identified that negative effects of abuse are greatest for females in the families in which high levels of stress are found (Kurtz *et al.*, 1993; Walker, 1979). Reports also demonstrate the influence of socio-cultural and family variables [e.g., socio-economic status (SES) and quality of the parent-child interaction] on negative outcome (Herrenkohl, Rupert, Egolf & Lutz, 1995).

Stress has received a major portion of blame for sewing as the catalyst that turns an unpleasant situation into an abusive one. Theories cannot fully explain domestic violence without the addition of the concept of stress that gives rise to maladaptive coping responses, because abusive partners are not violent under all, or even most circumstances. What seems to be responsible for aggravating the level of conflict between family members is not any particular type of stress but, rather the presence of a stress-filled environment, which may originate from a number of sources, especially in relation to socio-economic disadvantage mentioned earlier (Egeland, Breitenbucher & Rosenberg, 1980). The impact of any stressor depends to a large extent on the characteristics of the individual who must cope with the stressor.

Stressful events in the family affect each female in different and unique way. However, certain stressful situations trigger more intense stress reactions and consequences than others. Child abuse/Domestic violence is certainly among the worst and most intrusive forms of stress (on par with war, domestic violence, and inadequate shelter and clothing). It impinges directly on the child's/female's daily life, may be ongoing and unpredictable, and is often the result of actions or inactions of persons whom the child/female trusts and on whom they depend. However, even traumatic events such as abuse, neglect, emotional deprivation, and related forms of maltreatment do not affect children/females in a predictable, characteristic fashion. Rather, their impact depends on many factors, especially the child's/females make up and available supports (Zahn-Waxler, Cole, Welsh & Fox, 1995).

Stress is one of those forces of nature and humankind that can convert static conditions into dynamic, chaotic patterns. Physical abuse and neglect occur most often in the context of social and economic family deprivation, which can transform predisposed, high-risk partner into abusive or neglectful ones. The greater degree of stress in the social environment of the abusive perpetrator increases the probability that violence will surface as an attempt to gain control or cope with irritating, stressful events.

Thus, stress may appear in many different form for different individuals, and it can best be understood as events or demands that create an acute or chronic imbalance for the individual or the family system. This imbalance, in turn, is typically met by counter pressure from the individual's coping efforts to return himself or herself to a more comfortable state of equilibrium.

The conclusions drawn from studies of stress indicate that the negative or positive impact of a stressful event depends to a large extent on the degree of interruption and disarry set into motion by the event and on the presence of psychological and physical buffers that regulate the harshness of the stressor in tangible and intangible ways (Rutter, 1983). As additional stressors accumulate, females/children become less able to resist the harmful effects of stress which can lead to adaptational failure (Rutter, 1979; Sroufe, 1989). Pandey (2005) reported that high level of stress predicted, high incidence of child abuse. More specifically, abusive parents reported high feeling of stress than their non abusive counterparts.

Review of studies thus, indicate a close relationship between abuse and stress reactions, therefore this variable was selected for present study to investigate the linkage between life stress and incidence of domestic violence.

(3) Women Empowerment

During the last few decades women empowerment related issues has been recognized as the central theme in exploring the dynamics of family violences and determining status of women in India. It has been in the main focus of government agenda in general and for social psychological researches in particular. Studies focusing on empowerment process are multifaceted including psychological, organizational and community levels of analysis (Kulkarni, 2000; Mahadevan *et al.,* 2005; Pandey, 2001a; Swift & Levin, 1987; Zimmerman *et al.,* 1997).

Empowerment: The basic concept

'Empowerment' term is used in both senses; empowerment as a value orientation for working in the community and secondly, it is a theoretical model for understanding the process and consequences of efforts to control and influence over decisions that affects one's life, organizational function and the quality of life (Perkins & Zimmerman, 1995; Rappaport, 1984).

"Empowerment" refers to the equal opportunity and equal sharing of views by males and females in decision making. In fact the term "Women Empowerment" has different notions. It has various synonyms such as "Gender Equality for Women", "Modernization of Women", and "Empowerment of Women". The concept of empowerment is an elusive one encompassing within it a myriad of rights. But what does empowerment mean in real terms ? At what point can we say, we are "empowered"?

The role and empowerment of women have many facets or angles from which it is being tackled. Empowerment of women involves many things; economic opportunity, social equality, and personal rights. Three major areas of empowerment are: educational empowerment—to increase her awareness and capabilities to participate in society; economic empowerment—to decrease her dependency and increase her participation as an economically productive member of the family and society; and legal empowerment—to ensure that her rights and welfare are safeguarded, and to encourage her participation in various forums as an equal member of the society of humankind.

In the process of empowering women, worldwide efforts have also been made. It has been recognized through many international conferences as a basic human right—and also as imperative for national development, population stabilization and global well-being. In 1993, an international conference was organized in Montreal, Canada. Further in 1994, U.N. conference held in Cairo, globally accepted the concept of empowerment of women for maternal health and successful promotion of reproductive health. The Department of Women and Child Development (DWCD) made efforts to make women strong, aware and alert about their rights, health and social development. Apart from all the efforts to enhance the status of women, Indian women are still in the trap of discrimination and inequality in many spheres of life.

Economic Dependence and Lack of Empowerment: Lack of economic resources underlines women's vulnerability to violence and their difficulty in extricating themselves from a violent relationship. The link between violence and lack of economic resources and dependence is circular. On the one hand, the threat and fear of violence keeps women from seeking employment or at best, compels them to accept low paid, home-based exploitative labour. On the other hand, without economic independence, women have no power to escape from an abusive relationship. However, in some countries, women's increasing economic activity and independence is viewed as a threat which leads to increased male violence. This is particularly true when the male partner is unemployed and feels his power is undermined in the household.

Studies have also linked a rise in violence to destabilization of economic patterns in society. Macro-economic policies such as structural adjustment programmes, globalization and the growing inequalities have been linked to the increasing levels of violence in several regions. The transition periods in the countries of central and Eastern Europe and the former Soviet Union, with increases in poverty, unemployment, hardship, income inequalities, high stress and alcohol abuse have led to increased violence in society in general, and violence against women in particular. These factors also act indirectly to raise women's vulnerability by encouraging more risk taking behaviour, more alcohol and drug abuse, the breakdown of social support networks and the economic dependence of women on their partners.

Domestic Violence: A State of De-empowerment

Women and children have been victimized by male aggression particularly sexual aggression, across recorded history. During the last few decades researchers have begun to study this phenomenon systematically. The women have been a primary impetus in stimulating scientific attention (Brown & Ziefert, 1988). Initial studies and services focused mostly on victims assessing public and professional attitudes towards victims, developing treatment services and establishing incidence and prevalence rates. More recent studies have confronted the issues involved in attempting to prevent violence against women.

A woman can only empower herself, although organization and agencies around the world can play significant role in supporting this journey. Through empowerment, women can achieve resourceful life with freedom and autonomy to choose her career after late adolescence (18+), freely decide to marry and have small family size (1 or 2 children), live a healthy life following an appropriate life style and free from all discriminations (Mahadevan *et al.*, 2005). Women often feel inequality and empowerment supports them to be more aware of the unfair power relations they face, however, empowerment process differs in accordance with their age, race, caste, class, culture and other status. Women around the world, under represent the positions of power and decision making is linked to women's overall unequal status in society and to structural biases with political, economic, cultural and social system in society.

Despite this, from psychological perspective, Swift and Levin (1987) reviewed numerous researches related to women empowerment and categorized these studies under four stage process. The first stage covers the studies related to the prevention of dysfunctional outcomes in women; the second stage studies are about the empowerment of women consistent with the initial descriptive stage of the empowerment process; the third stage is concerned with some of the preventive interventions fit into promotion paradigms; and fourth stage includes the researches to mobilize resources for empowerment. A close perusal of these research studies suggest that women still face blantatory discriminative practices resulting in various forms of maltreatments within and outside the family and therefore, it is barely essential to empower them to make woman strong, self sufficient and independent.

Thus, the influence of marital conflict, life stress and empowerment on domestic violence was studied in present research investigation.

Impact of Domestic Violence on Children

Domestic Violence—Child Abuse Relationship

Researchers have shown their concern in studying the associations between exposure of domestic violence and child abuse and their impact on development of children. Researchers have identified that maltreated children and abused women come from the same homes. Recent reviews of studies across different settings and with different samples indicate that the co-occurrence of child abuse and spousal abuse is high. In an examination of nearly three dozen studies, reviewers found similar empirical findings: Between 30 per cent and 60 per cent of children whose mothers had experienced abuse were themselves likely to be abused (Edleson, 1999). According to recent literature reviews, there are nearly one million children who were identified by child protection services as victims of substantiated or indicated abuse or neglect and one million women who were physically assaulted within the past 12 months (Weithorn, 2001). Frequently, these women and children are in the same homes.

Fear for their children's safety is an ongoing concern for battered women. In a national study conducted by the Canadian Centre for Justice Statistics, women were six times more likely than men to report being afraid for their children (Johnson & Burge, 2001) when they were victims of domestic violence.

Abused Mothers as Poor Role Model

Family is the fundamental unit of children's socialization. Children learn powerful lessons from their parents including how to resolve conflict and how to cope with having their needs frustrated. Studies suggest that children may fail to learn how to moderate their emotions when they are exposed to their parents' anger and emotional outbursts (Cummings *et al.,* 1985). When children witness one parent inflicting abuse on the other, or using threats of violence to maintain control within a relationship, seeds are planted that may result in the cycle repeating itself. If a father believes that he is king of his castle and the children's mother is his servant, lessons on sex-role expectations are being passed on to the children.

Straus *et al.,* (1980) suggests that most batterers have themselves been exposed to their mothers' victimization in childhood. For younger siblings, the impact of inappropriate role models may be compounded within a family. Not only do these children have to cope with exposure to domestic violence but also they may be victimized by older siblings who have absorbed the lessons of violence. In fact, this sibling abuse may predict future violence in intimate relationships for both boys and girls (Elliott, Mullis, Pierce & Simonelli 2002).

Relationships between women and their children are profoundly affected by living with domestic violence, and that women are aware that their ability to fulfil the mandates of motherhood are compromised. Women are acutely aware how, within the ideology of motherhood and the family, they have failed, but they believe that within the acutely constraining context of domestic violence they have protected their children both from extensive knowledge of the violence and from premature loss of their family and home. Simultaneously, children try to protect their mothers from awareness of how much they know and of how unhappy they are. The consequent silence means that women are living with the illusion that they are staying for the sake of the children, whereas, children live with the burden of secretly wishing that their parents would separate. Children told that the violence and abuse made them feel sad and angry as well as frightened.

Whether or not a child is also a direct victim of abuse seems to be associated with the degree of harm experienced. Hughes *et al.* (1989) found that children who were both abused and exposed to D.V. exhibited the most severe problem behaviours, only witnessed group showed moderate problem symptoms, and a comparison, no exposure group showed the least symptoms. In one study, the children indicated that being abused, or both abused and exposed, had a greater negative impact—based on their self ratings of problems—than did witnessing adult domestic violence alone (McColsky, Figueredo & Koss, 1995). Gender appears to be another factor that affects the types of problems experienced. In general, boys have been shown to exhibit more frequent problems, especially those who were exposed to D.V.

Moderators of Exposure Consequences

Over the past decade, considerable research has been conducted that highlights the extensive impact of exposure to violence on children. (Geffner, Jaffe & Sudermann, 2000; Graham-Bermann & Edleson, 2001; Holden, Gaffner & Jouriles, 1998; Rossman *et al.,* 2000). The impact of the exposure of domestic violence is also moderated/mediated by numerous factors like; age and gender, as well as what is known about possible risk and protective factors. Children may be exposed to less severe and less frequent forms of spousal violence but be profoundly affected because of the presence of other risk factors such as isolation, learning disabilities, or self blaming. In short, each child is affected in a unique manner forced to cope with domestic violence in his or her family. Two children in the same family may respond very differently to the same level of violence, depending on a host of complicated interacting variables that are only beginning to appreciate.

Domestic Violence Leads to Child Abuse

It is presumed that perpetrators of women intended to harm their adult victims. However, it is less clear that batterers intend to victimize the children who witness battering. Children are sometimes used by perpetrators to coerce the other parent is some way in conjunction with a violent episode (Jaffe & Geffner, 1998; Jaffe, Poisson & Cunningham, 2001). Many children who observe interadult violence are injured either directly (intentionally) or indirectly (accidentally) during a violent episode. Exposure to domestic violence may be greater for young children (Wolak & Finkelhor, 1996). Under the Assault Replication Program (Fantuzzo et al., 1997) it was found that domestic violence occurred disproportionately in households with young children *i.e.* younger children (ages 0 to 5) were more likely to be exposed to multiple incidents of women abuse than older children. Studies suggest that abused women are twice as likely to abuse their children as non-abused women (Walker, 1984). In the context of domestic violence, however, male batterers reportedly abuse their children twice as often battered women. In one study girls whose mothers were battered, were 6.5 times more likely to be sexually abused than girls from non-violent families (Bowker *et al.*, 1988). Several studies on long term outcomes suggest that boys from violent families have a higher risk of using abusive tactics in their teenage and young adult relationship. A child's exposure to domestic violence is the single best predictor for transmitting violence across generations (Jaffe *et al.*, 1996).

When domestic violence occurs, the risk of physical and sexual abuse to children also increases dramatically, estimates vary from 30 per cent to 60 per cent regarding the frequency of the co-occurrence of physical abuse of children and domestic violence. Daughters of women who are assaulted by their partners are much more likely to be sexually abused in the home or by someone else. Mothers beaten by their partners are twice as likely to abuse their children and fathers who frequently beat their wives are more likely to beat their children (Straus & Gelles, 1990). Violence against an intimate puts children at risk, if the parent, usually, the mother is unable to protect the children from abuse and the effect of witnessing violence. The co-occurrence of domestic violence and child abuse represent a unique form of trauma, in which not only the child is harmed, but the person to whom the child would otherwise turn for comfort, support and safety is also being assaulted.

Risk and Protective Factors

Increasingly researchers are interested in accounting for individual differences when children are exposed to similar traumatic events. Risk and protective factors are essential elements in understanding the variability in children's behaviour. The research in risk and protective factors spans a wide range of traumas children may experience. Considerable research has been conducted on the dimensions of abuse as well as the discloser process and the response from supportive family members and community professional without oversimplifying the findings. The study suggests that impact of the abuse is moderated by factors inherent in the child (e.g. intelligence and temperaments), the family environment

Risk Factors	*Protective Factors*
• Presence of parental mental health challenges	• Supportive relationship with non abusive parent
• Presence of parental substance abuse	• Supportive relationship with an adult outside the immediate family
• Poverty and lack of access to resources (housing, economic support, legal assistance, counseling, employment) and child abuse	• Alternative role models· Success in academic, social or recreational pursuits.
• Family vulnerability (recent immigration, language and cultural barriers, visible minority status, parental-disabilities.	• Access to resources to support child and family (responses from the CAS and police that promote safety and healing).

(the presence of supportive adults, or the presence of other forms of maltreatment) and community response (the safety of the child and victimized parent is the priority for community services). In the same way, domestic violence occurs in the context of unique child characteristics, family dynamics and community resources.

To summarize, an understanding of the effect of domestic violence on an individual child will develop from an analysis of these risk and protective factors as well as the nature and severity of the violence. The problems in boys were categorized as externally oriented, such as hostility and aggression, while girls generally show evidence of more internally oriented problems, such as depression and somatic complaints (Carlson, 1991; Stagg, Wills & Howell, 1989).

Exposure to Domestic Violence and its Consequences

A sizeable number of studies report association between exposure to domestic violence and current child related problems or later adult problems (Emery, 1982; Griffiths, 1999; Grych & Fincham, 1990; Horn & Trickett, 1998; Paik & Comstock, 1994). Researchers evinced that even when children are not the direct targets of violence in the home, they can be harmed by witnessing the occurrence of such violence. The witnessing of domestic violence directly, or indirectly inferred, including cases in which child witness the aftermath of violence, such as cuts, bruises or broken limbs. Children who witness domestic violence can suffer severe emotional and developmental difficulties similar to children who are the direct victims of abuse. A child is exposed to domestic violence when an act that is defined as domestic violence, is committed in the presence of or witnessed by the child. The legal system is beginning to recognize the need to protect and care for these children. Exposure to violence on multiple levels can affect the parent's behaviour and can compound the effects on children. The number of studies on the impact of children's exposure to violence is still relatively limited due to various difficulties in conducting research on behavioural and emotional effects. For example, such research often possess ethical difficulties if it is to include a comparison or control group of children who are exposed to violence and not provided services to help mitigate this exposure.

Despite the limited research in this area, however, much can still be glanced from existing studies about the effects of children's exposure to domestic violence. The literature on family violence identifies adverse effects on children's physical, cognitive, emotional and social development.

1. On Life Span Development

Exposure to domestic violence may frequently co-occur with other risk factors such as poverty and its consequences, and other types of violence such as child maltreatment and community violence (Edleson, 1999b; Rudo, Powell, & Dunlap, 1998). This makes the unique effects of exposure to domestic violence hard to separate from those of other risks in a child's life. Sims, Hans and Cox (1996) found that when fathers were physically violent with mothers, infants were more likely to be insecurely attached to their mothers. Young children, because of their dependence, are particularly vulnerable to threats aimed at their mother, particularly when the source of those threats is another caregiver (father) and most especially when the children themselves are the target of such threats. Children are affected by violence exposure at all ages, less is known about the consequence of exposure at younger ages, especially any long-term consequences. Studies indicate the links between exposure to violence and negative behaviours in children across life span development.

(a) Prenatal: It is common for abuse to begin or continue during the time a women is pregnant. A 1993 survey by Statistics Canada found that 21 per cent of women abused by a marital partner were assaulted during pregnancy, and of these women 40 per cent reported that the abuse began during pregnancy (McFarlance, Parker, Soeken & Bullock, 1992, Rodgers, 1994). The full extent of effects of abuse on prenatal development and the intrauterine environment remain to be studied. However, women who are abused and beaten during pregnancy clearly suffer an elevated risk of injury to the fetus and complication during pregnancy and delivery.

(b) Birth to 2 Years: Even very young infants respond to witness parental conflict by stress that is measurable through heart rate, galvanic skin response (G.S.R.) and overt crying and distress (Cummings & Waxler, 1985). The effects of witnessing domestic violence, in addition to the negative effects on the mother's ability to focus on and care sensitively for her infant, can result in severe attachment problems and failure to thrive by the infant. Babies are also especially at physical risk during domestic violence, as they may be hit while in their mother's arms or near their mother or they may be thrown or hit by the abuser.

Perry (1995) studied the effects of violent environments on very young child. He reported that permanent negative changes in the child's brain and neural development occur when a child is exposed to abuse and other forms of violence at this age. Perry states that exposure to traumatic violence will alter the developing central nervous system, predisposing the individual to be more impulsive, reactive and violent behaviour. Some of behavioural results at later ages may include hyper vigilance to perceived threats and over responsively (aggression) when aggressive acts by others are anticipated. In the phases of infant and toddler development, existing research indicates clear associations between exposure to violence and emotional and behavioural problems. Infants and toddlers who witness violence either in their homes or in their community show excessive irritability, immature behaviour, sleep disturbance, emotional distress, fear of being alone and regression in toileting and language, exposure to trauma, especially violence in the family, interferes with a child's normal development of trust and later exploratory behaviours.

(c) Preschoolers: Preschoolers are severely distressed by witnessing domestic violence and conflict between their parents. Even relatively mild conflict causes children to cease playing and exploring, look distressed, seek proximity to their mother, and become very upset. Preschoolers who witness severe violence are often very clingy, have anxious attachments with their mothers, are difficult to manage, and are negative in their mood. Graham-Berman and Levendosky (1998) found preschoolers exposed to domestic violence to be more likely to express negative affect; to call other children names or insult them; and to bite, hit, or slap their peers during play interactions. Assessing trauma in preschool aged children is considered controversial because their symptoms may be quite different from adult who are diagnosed with PTSD (Post Traumatic Stress Disorder). For example these children are likely to show signs of hyper arousal, rather than symptoms of avoidance (Levendosky, Huth, Bocks, Semel & Shapiro, 2002).

(d) Aged 6 to 11 yrs (School Age Children): Children in the earlier school year often show their distress at witnessing domestic violence in aggressive and/or withdrawn behaviour at school and difficulty in concentrating at school (Jaffe *et al.*, 1990). These are the children who are often labeled with attention deficit disorder, without first being asked questions about what they are witnessing at home. Difficulties with peer relationship are often apparent, as well as low self-esteem and lack of energy for participation in school (Moore *et al.*, 1989). Boys may begin to be especially defiant with female teachers, mimicking the disrespect for women they see at home. Overall, children in this age group who are exposed to domestic violence tend to show both emotional and behavioural problems (Sternberg *et al.*, 1993), although individual children will vary in their symptoms severity because of factors such as frequency, severity and duration of violence witnessed, personality and family characteristics; and strengths and coping abilities.

(e) Adolescents: Adolescents who witness domestic violence may become truant at school because of anxiety and wanting to stay at home as a protector for the victimized parent. Some adolescents cope through alcohol and drug abuse or escape the family situation by running away from home. Involvement in juvenile delinquency occurs at an elevated rate. A lack of ability to focus on future plans is often present, together with an avoidance style of coping. Depression and suicide is another possibility at this age. Involvement with an antisocial peer group is common. The most common and specific indicator of exposure to domestic violence may be abusive dating relationship in adolescents who begin to practice what they have witnessed at home (Reitzel & Wolfe, 2001).

(f) Adults: Some research suggests long-term negative effects of exposure to domestic violence. Numerous studies have found that exposure to family violence in childhood predicts less positive adult's social adjustment (Henning, Leitenberg, Coffey, Turner & Bennett, 1996) and depression in adulthood (Straus, 1992). In our day to day life people confront with numerous adults who are still haunted by childhood memories of domestic violence. These individuals often disclose lifelong symptoms such as distrust of any intimate relationship and ongoing flashbacks and nightmares. The most common adult effect may be the cycle of violence which refers to the fact that childhood exposure to violence is one of the significant factors associated with domestic violence in adult years (Reitzel & Wolfe, 2001).

2. Behavioural and Emotional Disturbances

Researchers (Edleson, Jaffe & others, 1988) have also identified a host of behavioural, emotional and psychological difficulties associated with exposure to domestic violence. In general, studies suggest that exposure to parental violence is a form of psychological abuse and can be harmful to children both in the short term and over the life span. As with any other trauma or life stressor, how children are affected individually is dependent on a range of variables including their age, gender, the presence of other risk factors, and protective factor such as an extensive support system and access to resource that may reduce the harm they suffer (Rossman, Hughes & Rosenberg, 2000).

Emery (1982) did pioneering work to identify conflict as the active harmful ingredient for children coping with divorce. According to his research and that of other researchers, children show the greatest level of adjustment difficulties when their parents' separation is marked by conflict before, during and after the relationship ends, the concept that the divorce perse did not result in emotional and behavioural problems but rather, that the problems come from exposure to severe conflict.

Emotional Problems

Emotional (internalizing) problems such as anxiety, depression, low self esteem, withdrawal and lethargy are also noted in children who are exposed to family violence other children experience somatic complaints (bodily aches, pains and illness with not known medical cause). These symptoms may result because the children have a lot of internal tension with no effective way of addressing the problem expressing their feelings, or seeking help. Many observers have felt that internalizing problems along with a need to be perfectly behaved and an exaggerated sense of needing to help their mother are particularly common in girls, who witness family violence (Jaffe, Wolfe & Wilson, 1990; Kerig, Fedorowicz, Brown, Patenaude & Warren, 1998).

Children exposed to domestic violence may become aggressive with siblings, peers and teachers. They can be noncompliant, irritable and easily angered. Some children who destroy property and have a tendency to get into fights may develop more antisocial behaviour in their adolescence and end up in Juvenile Court as offenders.

Some studies have shown that children who witness domestic violence may be hampered in their social and school development (Moore, Pepler, Mae & Michele, 1989; Randolf & Talamo, 1997). Children who have been exposed to violence may be preoccupied with this issue and have difficulty in concentrating on school work. Their social development may be hampered because they are too sad, anxious, or preoccupied to participate in social activities. Some children may use aggressive strategies in interpersonal problem solving that may make them unpopular and rejected.

Numerous researchers have shown that many children who witness domestic violence suffer from PTSD (Post

Traumatic Stress Disorder). These children have been exposed to violence involving serious injury or death threats. The children's response involved acute fear, helplessness or horror, or in the case of younger children, agitated or disorganized behaviour. There may be a persistent avoidance of anything that reminds the child of the violence. Symptoms of increased arousal such as difficulty in falling asleep, irritability, outbursts of anger, difficulty in concentrating, hyper-vigilance and an exaggerated startle response may be present (American Psychiatric Association, 2000).

Lehmann (1997) found that 56 per cent of a sample of children in women's shelters met the full criteria for PTSD and the majority of the remaining children in the sample showed some symptoms associated with this disorder. Similarly, Graham-Berman & Levendosky (1998) evinced that 13 per cent of their sample of 64 children exposed to domestic violence qualified for a complete PTSD diagnosis. However, 52 per cent suffered from intrusive and unwanted remembering of the traumatic event(s), 19 per cent displayed traumatic avoidance and 42 per cent experienced traumatic arousal symptoms. Children with PTSD symptoms had significantly more internalizing behavioural problems and more externalizing problems than children without trauma symptoms (Graham-Bermann & Levendosky, 1998). Many children who are exposed to women abuse in their homes may never have known a calm and quiet environment even from their earliest childhood or infancy, and, thus their development and reactions are more chronically affected than those children who experience a single traumatic event in a peaceful and supportive environment.

Frequently, there are also more subtle symptoms related to children exposed to violence, such as inappropriate attitudes about the use of violence in resolving conflicts; inappropriate attitudes about violence against women; hyper-sensitivity about problems at home and a sense that they are to blame for the violence.

Numerous studies support a link between exposure to community violence and symptoms of anxiety, depression and aggressive behaviours in school-age children living in violent urban neighbourhoods. As with preschoolers, school-age children exposed to violence are more likely to show increases in sleep disturbance, and less likely to explore and play freely and to show motivation to master their environment. They often have difficulty paying attention and concentrating because they are distracted by intrusive thoughts. Other studies have reported that school age children who are exposed to family violence are affected similarly to those exposed to community violence. Such children often show a greater frequency of internalizing (withdrawal, anxiety) and externalizing (aggressiveness delinquency) behaviour problems in comparison to children from non-violent families. Overall functioning, attitudes, social competence and school performance are often affected negatively. In addition, studies show that as children get older, those who have been abused and neglected are more likely to perform poorly in school to commit crime; and to experience emotional problems, sexual problems and alcohol/substance abuse.

A cursory glance at review of literature on impact of domestic violence on children reveals that direct or indirect exposure to domestic violence has adverse consequences on cognitive, motivational and emotional development of children. Therefore, it was assumed that domestic violence may also have negative impact on behavioural functioning of children.

THE PRESENT STUDY

Domestic violence has emerged as a major psycho-social problem of present era. It is present at epidemic rate in the same or other forms throughout the world. Since antiquity, it is deeply rooted in Indian Society and has been witnessed in many forms (viz; Manasa—mental harassment, Vaccha—verbal harassment and 'Karmana'—physical assaults or torture). However, the phenomenon of domestic violence has always been either ignored or unnoticed because of the very personal/familial issue. As a result, very silently but rapidly crimes against women have taken place in our society in many forms ranged from physical assaults, psychological abuses, sexual assaults, economic abuses to infanticides, homicides or dowry deaths.

Domestic Violence (DV) is a widely studied area of research in developed countries. The findings of these researches have not only evinced the causative factors of D.V. but also have relevance for designing and implementing interventions to check this evil. A close perusal of these investigations reveals that most of the researches have been done from sociological perspective in which structural variables have been used to examine the nature and gravity of domestic violence across different strata of society, however, on the basis of such researches, causative explanations become difficult. Therefore, to understand the process of domestic violence, researches from psychological perspectives are essential, then only causal explanations can be made and the conceptualization of domestic violence will become easier. Furthermore, researches on domestic violence suffer from context specific methodological issues. Most of the studies are based on secondary data or survey reports and these studies might have suffered from reporting biases. Another relevant point is that a numerable number of researches are conducted in western countries where domestic violence was recognized as a great social evil in 1980s in U.S.A. and was considered a National Emergency and preventive interventions have been proliferated since the last few decades in these countries.

Therefore, it is quite natural that the nature and gravity of 'Domestic Violence' in India will largely differ from that of developed countries and therefore, such issues should be investigated in relation to contextual and cultural variations. Although, the incidence rate of D.V. is very high in Indian society yet the correct identification of abused cases is very difficult due to multifaceted reasons. Despite this, a great concern has been shown by government organizations (National Commission for Women), women organizations, professionals (law, court, police etc.), media and above all researchers concerning different disciplines to explore the causes and consequences of domestic violence and to develop preventive strategies to counteract this evil.

A cursory glance at review of researches indicates that domestic violences is a extensively studied area in sociological researches. This phenomenon has been studied in relation to numerous sociological factors like; patriarchy, family dynamics, social status, socio-cultural factors, education, occupation and economic conditions (poverty and unemployment etc.). Despite this, there are numerous questions still unanswered concerning the social dynamics of D.V. and its consequences on women and children.

Psychological Dynamics of Domestic Violence

Apart from sociological factors, a comprehensive understanding of the psychological dynamics of domestic violence is essential to assess the process of violent actions against women behind the closed doors. Although, psychologists have made meager efforts to study this phenomenon, however, a close perusal of available psychological researches on domestic violence evinces the role of socialization, gender preferences and value system, perception and attitude of society towards D.V., in the emergence and sustenance of domestic violence. Yet, the role of intervening variables i.e., cognitive, affective and interactional factors in the origin of domestic violence and its consequences on women and children, should be studied thoroughly.

A cursory glance at review of literature points out some unexplored dimensions of domestic violence;

(i) Understanding the variations witnessed across different contexts and strata of society;
(ii) Knowing the gap between concept and experiential reality;
(iii) Identifying the background, causality and consequences of D.V.;
(iv) Readdressing the changes in the nature and gravity of Domestic Violence etc.

In this backdrop present study was planned to investigate the psycho-social dynamics of domestic violence and its impact on children. Keeping in view, some research questions have been raised, concerning the proposed study:

1. What are the trends and patterns of domestic violence in rural and urban communities?
2. Which background/contextual factors play pervasive role in the emergence and sustenance of domestic violence?
3. What are the prominent social factors which play causative roles in the incidence of domestic violence?
4. What are the roles of psychological variables in the origin and sustenance of domestic violence?
5. What are the consequences of exposure to domestic violence on children?
6. What recommendations should be made on the basis of findings of the present study?

Objectives and Hypothesis

Objectives of the Study

Based on the research questions raised above, this study was carried out with following objectives:

1. To find out the patterns and trends of domestic violence in rural and urban areas of Gorakhpur region.
2. To identify social factors which provide germane grounds to domestic violence?
3. To explore the role of psychological factors in the origin of domestic violence.
4. To establish the linkages between domestic violence and child abuse, and;
5. To investigate the impact of exposure to domestic violence on behavioural functioning of children.

Hypotheses

On the basis of research objectives, following hypotheses were formulated. It was hypothesized that;

1. The patterns and trends of domestic violence will differ at some extent in rural and urban communities.
2. Certain socio-demographic factors like; age, education, socio-economic status (S.E.S,.) occupation, caste, family structure, would also be linked with domestic violence.
3. The extent of domestic violence would also be influenced by marital conflict, life stress and women empowerment.
4. Domestic violence would be found positively related to child abuse and the high incidence of child abuse would be predicted by various forms of domestic violence, and
5. The exposure of domestic violence would exert negative impact on behavioural functioning of children. Furthermore, the domestic violence and child abuse would contribute inversely to the behavioural functioning of children.

2

Method

Plan and Strategy of the Study

In this chapter, despite the methodological problems involved in the study of domestic violence, the plan and strategy of present research have been discussed. For screening the cases of domestic violence and to finalize the measures, a preliminary study was conducted. Apart from this, an attempt has also been made to present an overview of universe and sample characteristics, research strategies of antecedent, mediating and outcome variables, selected in the proposed study.

Research Strategy

The dynamics of domestic violence are multifaceted concerning environmental, demographic, socio-cultural and psychological factors. Domestic violence may take place at multiple points as a result of multi causative factors. It is conceptualized as a Social-Psychological phenomenon and multiple forces determine it at four different ecological levels; the individual (ontogenetic), the family (the micro-system), the community (the exo system), and the culture (the macro-system), in which both the individual and family are interconnected with each other.

The agents of domestic violence (Perpetrators) are found within and outside the family. Perpetrators may be husband (spouse), family members, relatives, neighbours, and any significant member for the women. The incidence rates of domestic violence in eastern districts of U.P. are observed in plenty; however, correct statistics of cases are under-estimated due to methodological problems in the assessment of domestic violence. Therefore, in the present study, multiple criteria were adapted for the screening of abused cases ; (i) Primary data based on Self Report Measures; and (ii) Secondary data or Reported cases.

Primarily, to identify the pattern and trends of domestic violence in Gorakhpur region, registered or reported cases of domestic violence were identified from authentic sources viz; formal organizations, family court, women organization, police records, local hospitals etc. These reports provided firsthand or fundamental information about the pattern and trend of domestic violence. Despite this, these information helped to design an in depth household study based on primary data to investigate the "Psycho-social Dynamics of Domestic Violence and its Impact on Children", on a numerable number of women and children of rural-urban areas belonging to different strata of society.

Subject selection procedure was used to determine the levels of domestic violence, child abuse and other characteristics like; gender, age, socio-economic status of the respondents. According to D. Amato, (1970), "In an experimental study, use of classificatory factor is an accepted technique of experimentation." Calfee, (1975) also confirms that the major experimental variable has to be considered as classificatory factor. This procedure is extensively exercised in a sizable number of psychological researches (Berry, 1976; Misra & Tripathi, 1980; Pandey, 2005). Since the participants of present study were women and children (7-14 years) thus, some of the variables were investigated on females while certain other variables were investigated on their children. Variables and concerned measures, administered on females are displayed in Table 2.1.

Similarly, studied variables and measures administered on children are presented in Table 2.2.

Table 2.1: Shows variables along with their measures administered on females.

S.No.	*Variables*	*Measures*
1.	Domestic violence: Physical Psychological, Sexual and Economic abuses.	(i) Domestic Violence Checklist (S. Pandey, 2006) (ii) Domestic Violence Interview Schedule (S. Pandey, 2006)
2.	Environmental factors:	
	Rural-urban setting	Personal Data Sheet (PDS) (S. Pandey, 2006)
	Family Structure	Personal Data Sheet (PDS) (S. Pandey, 2006)
3.	Social-status; (caste, education and socio-economic status), Age, Health status etc.	Personal Data Sheet (PDS) (S. Pandey, 2006)
4.	Psychological Factors:	
	1. Marital Conflict	Marital Conflict Scale (Eggeman *et. al.* 1985; adapted by S. Pandey, 2006)
	2. Stress	Life Stress Scale (Modified version of Holmes & Rahe, 1967 adapted by S.Pandey, 2002)
	3. Empowerment	Empowerment Questionnaire (S. Pandey, 2006)

Table 2.2: Displays variables along with measuring tools, administered on children.

S.No.	*Variables*	*Measures*
1.	Child abuse and neglect	Child Abuse Checklist (S. Pandey, 2002; 2005)
2.	Social-status; (caste, socio-economic status), Child-age, gender, education, birth order, health status etc.	Personal Data Sheet (PDS) (S. Pandey, 2006)
3.	1. Child behaviours	Child Behaviour Questionnaire (S. Pandey, 2006)
	2. Aggression	Aggression Questionnaire (G. C. Pati, 1976)

Screening of the Study Setting and Selection of Participants

Settings of the study from where sample was drawn consisted of rural and urban areas of Gorakhpur region. Of course, Uttar Pradesh is ranked one of the most backward states of the country however, it stands first in population density (Total Population of U.P., 16,61,74,612; Male: 8,75,60,236; Female: 7,86,14,376) as compared to total population of India (Total = 1,02,70,15,274; Male: 53,12,77,078; Female: 49,57,38,169).

According to 2001 census report, in Uttar Pradesh, birth rate is 23.8 and death rate is 10.3 per thousand. The development level is also very low as compared to many other states and per capita income is almost unchanged. The literacy rate is also low in U. P. (Total literacy = 57.36%, male literacy = 70.23%, female literacy = 42.98%) as compared to the literacy rate of India (Total literacy = 68.38%, male literacy = 75.85% and female literacy = 54.16%). The average landholding is also very low as compared to other states. The industrial development and productivity are also unsatisfactory. Apart from this, medical and transport facilities are inadequate in rural areas. The physical features and socio-demographic characteristics of the region indicated the appropriateness of setting for the investigation, thus, present study was conducted in rural and urban areas of Gorakhpur region. The majority of population in this district is rural and illiterate. The other characteristics of rural-urban settings are not homogenous and numerous environmental and socio-cultural variations are also observed in both setting.

The rural population has traditional family structure (joint-family pattern) than urban population. Apart from this, they are deprived of various facilities viz., schooling, communication channels, transportation facilities, health and family welfare centers and sources of work force whereas, urban setting enjoys all these facilities. However, no sharp variation was found regarding composition of caste, community, and status of woman harassments and abuse child (Table 2.3). Apart from this, the cases of domestic violence are witnessed very often in eastern districts of U.P. These features provided appropriate setting for the study of domestic violence.

Table 2.3: Displays cases of domestic violence in Gorakhpur and nearby districts of U.P. (year 2006).

Districts	*Forms of abuses*		
	Dowry Deaths	*Physical Harassments*	*Sexual Harassments*
Gorakhpur	15	58	19
Deoria	17	15	03
Kushinagar	22	11	09
Maharajganj	10	08	17
Basti	11	Not available	09
Sant Kabir Nagar	07	Not available	04
Siddhartha Nagar	19	10	04
Total	101	102	65

Research Design: The study followed a 2X2X3 factorial design with two level of residential setting (rural-urban) X abuse level (abused-nonabused) X socioeconomic status (high, middle and low). However the study is correlational in nature, thus, correlation and regression analysis would also be exercised.

Participants: A total of 140 families (comprised of women and children) were randomly selected from rural and urban areas of Gorakhpur district.. Later on 20 cases of child were dropped as they were too young to respond on self report measures. Finally, 140 women and 120 children participated in present study. Further, on the basis of median score (mdn= 148), obtained on Domestic Violence Checklist, females were divided into abused and non-abused groups. The cases of abused and non-abused are displayed in Table 2.4. This table displays the categorization of sample in accordance with different group of woman and children. It is evident from the table, a total of 64 cases were found highly abused and 56 cases were identified as low or non-abused. Similarly, children, either exposed to domestic violence or unexposed were also identified on the basis of reports given by mothers. The Child Abuse

Checklist was used for screening the cases of child abuse (mdn =115). As Table 2.4 denotes, 56 cases were found abused and 64 cases were identified as non-abused.

Table 2.4: Categorization of sample according to the level of domestic violence, child abuse, environmental setting, age, caste and socio-economic status.

Number of respondents according to:	*Women (mothers) (cases of violence)*	*Children (cases of abuse)*
Domestic Violence/Child Abuse:		
Abused	64	56
Non abused	56	64
Environmental Setting:		
Rural	70	60
Urban	70	60
Age: 46 Yrs. +	6	7-10 yrs
36—45	32	11-14 yrs
26—35	84	
Below 25	19	Gender: Boys = 60
Gender: Only Females	140	Girls = 60
Caste:		
General	84	84
OBC	43	43
SC	14	14
Community:		
Hindu	80	70
Muslim	60	50
Socio-economic Status (SES):		
High	42	40
Middle	48	40
Low	51	40

The background characteristics of women and their children were determined on the basis of Personal Data Sheet (PDS).

Demographic information about the participants (women) belonging to rural and urban areas of Gorakhpur district are displayed in Tables 2.5 and 2.6 respectively. The mean age of urban women (Mean age = 32.39 yrs) is greater than rural women (Mean age = 30.76 yrs). A little variation is also

Table 2.5: Demographic information of the respondents belonging to rural area of Gorakhpur Region

Age variation Forms of Domestic of the victims of Domestic Violence	*Length of Marriage*	*Caste Composition and Socio-economic Status*	*Education Status*	*Female's (Victim's) Employment*	*Occupation*	*Husband's Violence (Abuses)*
20 Yrs. to 55 Yrs. 20-25 Yrs. 25-30 Yrs. 30-35 Yrs. 35+ Mean Age = 30.76 Yrs.	**5 Months to 31 Yrs. Within 5 Yrs. 5-10 Yrs. 10-15 Yrs. 15+ Mean Marital Duration = 13.35 Yrs.**	**Community: Hindu and Muslim Caste: General, OBC and SC Socio-economic Status: High, Middle and Low**	**Illiterate = 38% Educated = 62% Upto 5th Class = 4.23% 8th Class = 21% Intermediate = 31% Graduate + = 5.64%**	**House-hold Labour + Farmer Business Class Teacher and Other Services**	**Unemployed Labour Farmer Teacher Student Business Private Services Government Services**	**Physical abuse, Sexual Psychological and Economic abuses Other Forms of Abuses: *i.e.,* Dowry, harassments, Bride burning homicides, infanticides, etc.**

Table 2.6: Demographic information of the respondents belonging to urban area of Gorakhpur Region

Age variation of victims	*Length of Marriage*	*Caste Composition and Socio-economic Status*	*Education Status*	*Female's (Victim's) Employment*	*Husband's Occupation*	*Forms of Domestic Violence (Abuses)*
21 Yrs. to 56 Yrs. 20-25 Yrs. 25-30 Yrs. 30-35 Yrs. 35+ Mean Age = 32.39 Yrs.	**4 Months to 38 Yrs. Below 5 Yrs. 5-10 Yrs. 10-15 Yrs. Above 15 Yrs. Mean Marital Duration = 14.06 Yrs.**	**Community: Hindu and Muslim Caste: General, OBC and SC Socio-economic Status: High, Middle and Low**	**Illiterate = 21.43% Educated = 78.57% Up to 5th Class = 8.57% Up to 8th Class = 8.57% Intermediate = 28.5% Graduate + = 32.86%**	**Household Labour Business Teacher Other Government Services Private Services**	**Labour Teacher Advocate Business Government Services (Police, Army, Railway etc.) Private Services (Sales-representative, Agents etc.)**	**Physical Sexual Psychological Economic Other Forms of Abuses: *i.e.,* Dowry, harassments, homicides, infanticides, Induced abortion etc.**

observed in mean length of marital duration (M(U) = 14.06 Vs (R) = 13.35 yrs). The caste composition of both settings is almost similar. However, a clear cut variation was found in education status. In rural sample 62 per cent participants were educated and 38 per cent were illiterate whereas in urban sample, 78.57 per cent women were found educated and 21.43 per cent were uneducated. However, majority of urban women were found highly educated (graduate + = 32.80%) than rural women (graduate + = 5.64%). Majority of rural women were household than urban sample. Similarly a sharp variation was observed on husband's occupation. A sizable no. of males (husband) were either unemployed or farmers in rural sample whereas in urban sample the occupation of husband ranged from service class, (Govt. and Private services), business to labour class respectively. The influence of socio-economic conditions and caste composition on incidence of domestic violence is also very clearly identified from the Tables. Tradition ridden higher caste families were also found abusive. However, maximum number of cases of D.V. were identified from lower caste (S/C) and Muslim Community. It appears that domestic violence is an universal phenomenon which is witnessed in each and every strata of society with little variations in its form and intensity.

Measures

A set of measuring tools were used in the present study. Keeping in view the suitability of participants and appropriateness of measuring tools, a set of measures were carefully selected or developed and therefore, Pilot study was conducted. This preliminary study was quite beneficial in many ways (i) firstly, the problems occurring in conduction of the study and administering various tools were identified. It was noticed that Domestic Violence Checklist was sensitive enough to tap the important aspects of psychological functions, therefore, it was planned to administer this Checklist, at the end of the first session. Meanwhile, participants would have developed smooth relationship and faith in the investigators, who have already established rapport and warm association with participants. While collecting data in rural setting, the medium of instruction was adopted either Hindi or Bhojpuri (local dilect) to solve the problems of communicating instruction and items in understandable terms. A set of measures were applied on females whereas, certain measures were administered on children. A brief description of these measures, is given below:

Measures Administered on Women

1. Personal Data Sheet (P.D.S.): In order to determine the socio-demographic and familial characteristics of women and children Personal Data Sheet (Pandey, S., 2006) was used (Appendix II).

2. Domestic Violence Interview Schedule: Domestic violence interview schedule was used to asses perception, practices and trends of violence behind closed doors (D.V.) in different strata of society. This interview schedule was also used for the determination of case histories of the abused victims. This schedule contains two sections: A and B. Section A includes items related to general trend of D.V. whereas, section B involves items related to occurrence of D.V. in personal cases. Since items of the schedule are open-ended, therefore respondents had freedom to answer each items in own narratives (Appendix-III). This Interview Schedule is Pilot tested.

Scoring: Since responses were given in statement, so content analysis and other qualitative techniques were used to determine the trend and causative factors of D.V.

3. Domestic Violence Checklist: To ascertain the intensity and forms of domestic violence *i.e.* physical abuse, psychological abuse, sexual abuse and economic abuse, Domestic Violence Checklist (developed by Pandey, S., 2006) was used.

In Pilot study, try out was done to gain insight about the appropriateness of language and suitability of the items. A close perusal of the responses given on items suggested that some of the items were either irrelevant or ambiguous, therefore, these items were dropped out of the final set and ultimately 89 items were retained in the Checklist (shown in Appendix-IV). The reliability (r =.89) and validity (r = .71) of the Checklist were found highly significant.

Scoring: Responses on each item were scored following 4, 3, 2 and 1 order. Total summated scores in each area denote the magnitude of abuse in specific area and on the basis of the grand total, abuse as a whole was determined.

4. Marital Conflict Scale: This scale is originally developed by Eggeman *et al.* (1985) and adapted by Pandey, S. (2006). To determine the level of conflict between husband and wife this scale was used. Marital Conflict Scale contains a total of 27 items comprised on 17 positive and 10 negative items (Appendix-V).

Scoring: Responses given on positive items were scored following 5, 4, 3, 2 and 1 and negative items were scored on 1, 2, 3, 4 and 5 pattern. Total score denotes the level of conflict between husband and wife.

5. Life Stress Scale: This is a modified version of Holmes and Rahe (1967) Readjustment scale (Pandey, 2002). This measure consists of 29 items pertaining to stressful events. The scale was used to measure the feeling of stress in participants.

Scoring: The scoring was done following 4, 3, 2 and 1 order. Total summated scores indicate magnitude of stress in females. Reliability of this measure was found high (r = .76). High scores indicate high level of stress in respondents whereas, low scores denote low level of stress in females. (Appendix-VI).

6. Women Empowerment Questionnaire: This questionnaire is developed by Pandey, S. (2006), to assess the empowerment level of women related to familial, educational social, political, economic and personal concerns. The questionnaire consists of 30 items. The reliability (r = .87) and validity (r = .69) of the questionnaire were found high.

Scoring: Responses given on items were scored following 5, 4, 3, 2 and 1 order. Total summated scores denote the empowerment level of females. (Appendix-VII).

Measuring Tools Administered on Children

1. Personal Data Sheet (P.D.S.): In order to determine the socio-demographic and familial characteristics of children, Personal Data Sheet (Pandey, S. 2006) was used.

2. Child Abuse Checklist: This checklist is developed and standardized by Pandey, S. (2005) to determine the child's physical, psychological, and sexual abuses and child neglect concerning; physical, emotional and educational area. The Checklist contains 150 items related to different forms of abusive treatments by parents/family members or any significant others and children are asked to respond on a 4-point scale, given in front of each item (Appendix-VIII).

Scoring: Responses on each item were scored following 3, 2, 1 and 0 order. Total summated scores in each area denote the magnitude of abuse and neglect in specific area and on the basis of the grand total, abuse as a whole was determined.

3. Child Behaviour Questionnaire: This questionnaire was developed to assess various forms of behavioural functioning of children. The Checklist includes 10 areas of behaviour patterns i.e.; helping behaviour, social interaction, non-compliance, destructive behaviour, affection, discipline, reciprocal relationship, task involvement, bullying and study behaviour concerned with positive and negative patterns of behaviour (Appendix-IX). Reliability (r = .89) and validity (r = .78) of the questionnaire were found high.

Scoring: Responses of each item were scored following 4, 3, 2 and 1 order. Total summated scores in each area indicate different forms of behavioural functioning in children.

4. Aggression Questionnaire: To determine the level of aggression in children, Aggression Questionnaire developed by G. C. Pati (1976) was used. This scale includes 16 situations with 3-point closed-end scale. The responses obtained on each item are transformed into standard scores. Higher scores denote more aggression. The reliability and validity of the test are reported high (Appendix-X).

Procedure

Since screening of study settings and identification of cases were already done in preliminary phase of the study, hence on the basis of reported data, the research team approached to the respective areas of the study and tried to establish rapport with the family members. This study was conducted in rural and urban areas of Gorakhpur district, thus, research team visited these places one by one. Prior to this, a brief orientation session, to introduce the nature and purpose of the study and detailed instruction about administration of measuring tools, was organized by project director because high degree of skill and ingenuity on part of the research team was essential to communicate the respondents in effective manner. The sample of this investigation consisted of females and/or their children, thus multiple phases for data collection were required. Since, availability of subjects for the study was a difficult problem because sample characteristics differed on degree of environmental setting (rural-urban), age (25-45), caste (general, OBC and SC), community (Hindu-Muslim), socio-economic status (high, middle and low) and level of abuses. So, it was quite difficult to approach the respondents and schedule them for administration of the measuring tools, yet, efforts were made to contact the females and their children in different settings. The study was conducted into two phases.

First Phase of the Study

First of all, women were contacted for this investigation. This phase required multiple sessions.

Ist Session: In this session, women were contacted either at home or work place (in case of working women). They were explained about the nature and purpose of the study in effective manner and proper rapport was established. They were given 'Personal Data Sheet' to get background records. Then, to identify the general pattern of 'Domestic Violence', women were interviewed with the help of Domestic Violence Interview Schedule and at the end of first session, they were given 'Domestic Violence Checklist'. Women were requested to respond on self report measures. As they completed responses, data were collected and they were thanked for their participation and further, they were requested to participate in 2nd session of the study.

IInd Session: In this session, psychological measures i.e., Marital Conflict Scale, Empowerment Questionnaire and Life

Stress Scale were given to the females and were requested to respond on these measures one by one. After completing the responses, women were thanked for their cooperation.

Second Phase of the Study

In the next phase of the study one of the children (exposed to domestic violence) of abused victim was contacted in school or at workplace (in case of child labour). An equal no. of children, who were not exposed to domestic violence were also selected as non-exposed group and then all children were requested to participate. Researcher explained about the nature and purpose of the study in effective manner and proper rapport was established, then, they were given a booklet containing Personal Data Sheet (PDS) and Child Abuse Checklist. Children were requested to respond on these measures one by one. As they completed responses on above said measures, data were collected and children were thanked for cooperation and were requested to participate in 2nd session of the study.

IInd Session: In the second session, children were given 'Child Behaviour Questionnaire' and 'Aggression Questionnaire' respectively. They were requested to respond on these measures. As they completed their responses, data were collected and children were thanked for participation.

Data obtained on various measures were scored according to rules, given in manuals. The obtained scores were treated for computer analysis.

Third Phase of the Study

This section dealt with case histories of a total of 12 extreme cases of domestic violence. The Domestic Violence Interview Schedule was used to determine the case histories of abused women from different strata of society. The narratives given by respondents were recorded and have been reported in the second section of the result in (chapter-3).

3

Results

Present chapter contains the results obtained from statistical analyses of the data. At the out set, the scores for the analysis were determined on the basis of responses given by the respondents (women and children) of rural and urban settings belonging to different strata of society. Responses on various measures were scored according to defined rules. The statistical treatments of scores were done in terms of Comparative (ANOVA and t-test), Correlational and Step-Wise Multiple Regression (SWMR) analyses respectively. Apart from this, qualitative analysis was also applied to provide a vivid picture of the process, causative factors and consequences of domestic violence.

First section of the chapter deals with findings based on Quantitative Analysis. In this section, comparative analysis (ANOVA and t-test), Correlational Analysis and Step-Wise Multiple Regression (SWMR) Analysis have been exercised and reported. Second section of the Chapter contains 'Case Histories' based on qualitative analysis. The organization of findings has been done in accordance with major objectives of the study:

SECTION I: QUANTITATIVE ANALYSIS

I. Contextual Variations in the pattern and trends of domestic violence:

First objective of the study was to find out the patterns and trends of domestic violence in rural and urban communities of Gorakhpur region.

In order to determine the pattern as well as and trends of domestic violence in rural and urban communities, statistical treatments were done for the responses given by women of both communities, on Domestic Violence Checklist and Interview Schedules I and II.

A. Pattern of Domestic Violence in Rural—Urban Communities

The pattern of domestic violence across both the rural and urban settings was determined on the basis of scores obtained on D.V. Checklist. Results are displayed in Table 3.1. Likewise, the trend of D.V. in both settings was identified on the basis of responses obtained on Interview Schedule. Results are displayed in Tables 3.2, 3.3, 3.4 and 3.5 respectively.

Table 3.1: Shows Means and Weighted Means, SDs and F 'values' of various forms of domestic violence in different environmental setting.

Environmental Setting	*Type of D.V. (Abuses)*	*Physical Abuse*	*Sexual Abuse*	*Psychological Abuse*	*Economic Abuse*	*Abuse as a whole*
Rural	Mean	37.51	15.90	77.50	14.87	145.87
	WM	150.04	190.80	232.53	178.44	751.81
	SD	12.25	5.14	21.66	6.15	38.40
Urban	Mean	42.45	17.23	80.04	16.55	155.84
	WM	169.80	206.76	240.12	198.60	815.28
	SD	16.31	6.86	25.38	8.30	50.92
	F –'Values'	4.35*	1.77	.43	1.95	1.81

** P< .01
* P< .05

Table 3.1 shows Means, SDs and F-values of various forms of abuses reported by rural and urban females. A close perusal of results displayed in the Table 3.1 and Fig. 3.1 reveals that except physical abuse other forms of abuses did not vary significantly across both settings. However, significant F value for Physical abuse [$F(1, 149) = 4.35$, $P < .05$] indicates that women from urban areas were reported to be high victims of Physical abuse ($M = 42.45$) than women from rural areas

(M = 37.51), use of liquor, marital conflict and deterioration in value system are some of the salient reasons of high incidence of D.V. in urban culture. Wife beating is a common phenomenon particularly in urban community. Present result thus, suggests that D.V. is an universal problem and is present in both settings at high rate.

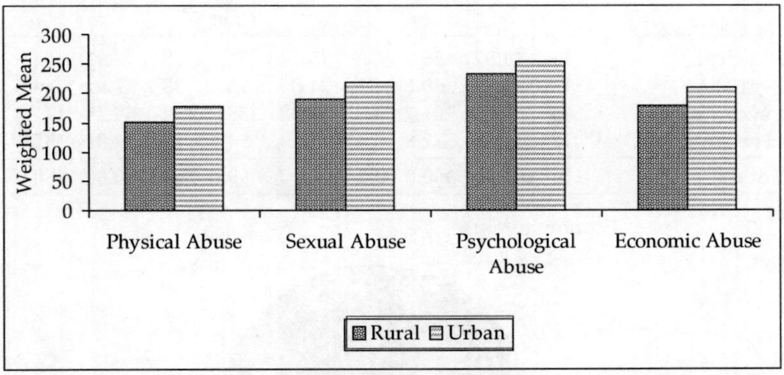

Fig. 3.1: Displays Domestic Violence (abuses) as a function of rural-urban environmental setting.

B: Trend of Domestic Violence

Further, in order to determine the trend of Domestic-violence (abuses) in rural and urban communities, women were interviewed on a structured interview schedule of domestic violence. The various forms of abuses as reported by women were calculated and the number of cases, victimized to various forms of abuse, were determined and transformed into percentages for total sample as well as for rural and urban population separately. Results displayed in Table 3.2 and Fig. 3.2(a) indicate that in case of total population the majority of women reported as victims of psychological abuse (49.25%) at a very high rate, followed by physical abuse (17.91%), sexual abuse (17.91%) and economic abuse (14.93%) respectively [Fig. 3.2(a)].

However, little variation on trend of D.V. was found across rural and urban settings. The number of cases on various forms of domestic violence differed across rural and urban

Table 3.2: Shows proportional distributions of domestic violence in rural and urban areas of Gorakhpur Region

Type of D.V. (Abuses)	*Rural*			*Urban*			*Total*		
	Frequencies	*%*	*Angular Proportion*	*Frequencies*	*%*	*Angular Proportion*	*Frequencies*	*%*	*Angular Proportion*
Physical	18	15.52	55.9	30	19.74	71	48	17.91	64.5
Sexual	16	13.79	49.6	32	21.05	75.8	48	17.91	64.5
Psychological	65	56.03	201.7	67	44.08	158.7	132	49.25	177.3
Economic	17	14.66	52.8	23	15.13	54.5	40	14.93	53.7
Total	116	100.00	360.0	152	100.00	360.0	268	100.00	360.0

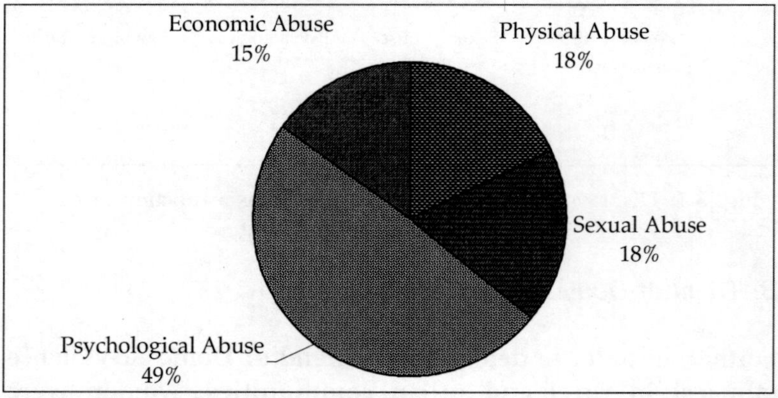

Fig. 3.2(a): Displays proportional distribution of the cases of domestic violence (abuses) in total sample.

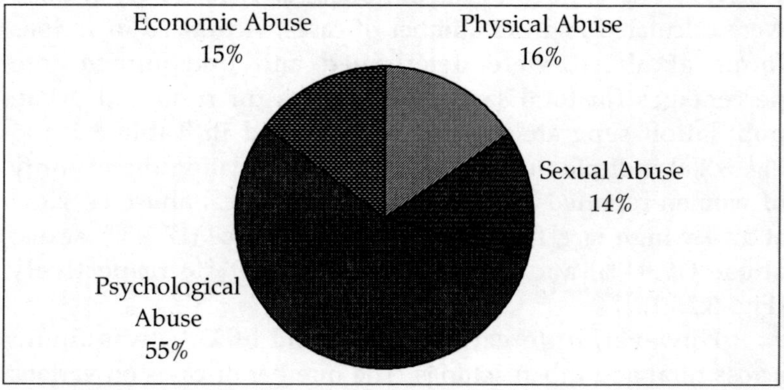

Fig. 3.2(b): Displays proportional distribution of the cases of domestic violence (abuses) in rural setting.

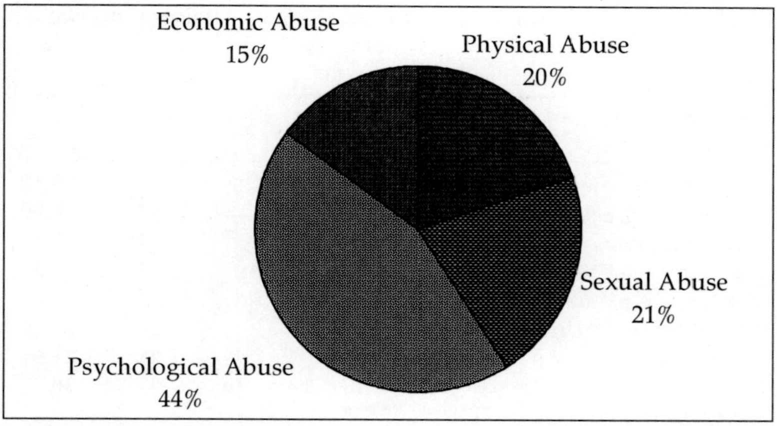

Fig. 3.2(c): Displays proportional distribution of the cases of domestic violence (abuses) in urban setting.

communities. Table 3.2 and Fig. 3.2(b) show the trend of domestic violence in rural setting. Rural women reported very high level of psychological abuse (56.03%) followed by physical abuse (15.52%), economic abuse (14.66%) and sexual abuse (13.79%) respectively whereas, the pattern of domestic violence in urban areas was different at some extent. Table 3.2 and Fig. 3.2(c) indicate that in urban setting majority of women reported victims of psychological abuse (44.08%) followed by sexual abuse (21.05%), physical abuse (19.75%) and economic abuse (15.13%) respectively. In other words, urban women were found less psychologically abused (44.08%) than rural women (56.03%). However, urban women were found more physically and sexually abused than rural women.

C: Causative Factors of Domestic Violence in Rural-Urban Communities

(i) Causes of Domestic Violence (Total Sample): Respondent's percentages for their reporting of the main causes of domestic violence were determined with the help of Domestic Violence Interview Schedule. Responses were content analyzed. The main causes of violence reported by respondents of both settings (total sample) are indicated in Table 3.3.

Table 3.3: Displays Main Causes of Domestic Violence in Total Sample.

Sl. No.	*Causes (reported)*	*Frequency*	*Percent-ages(%)*
1.	Alcohol/chewing tobacco	27	38.17
2.	Conflict between husband and wife	25	36.90
3.	Economic scarcity or Lack of money	23	32.54
4.	Embarrassing behaviour against women by family members	22	31.27
5.	Husband's Unemployment	20	28.29
6.	Dowry	18	25.51
7.	Attitudinal differences and conflicts between family members	17	20.78
8.	Ego clashes with in-laws	14	19.79
9.	Illiteracy	12	17
10.	Lottery or gambling	11	16.98
11.	Extra Marital Affairs	10	15.57
12.	Authoritative behaviour by husband and in-laws	10	15.56
13.	Infertility or having only girl child and no son	6	8.55
14.	Misunderstanding between family members	5	8.52
15.	Ignorance of husband and in-laws	4	8.49
16.	Mistrust by husband and in-laws	3	5.68

As is apparent from the table, that Alcohol/chewing tobacco is the main cause of domestic violence as 38.17 per cent victims reported this factor as a primary cause of physical abuse and assaults. Other main causes in preferential order are: conflict between husband and wife (36.90%), economic scarcity or lack of money (32.54%), embarrassing behaviour against women by family members (31.27%), husband's unemployment (28.29%), dowry (25.51%), attitudinal differences and conflicts between family members (20.78%), ego clashes with in-laws (19.79%), illiteracy (17%), lottery or gambling (16.98%), extra marital affairs (15.57%) and authoritative behaviour by husband and in-laws (15.56%), infertility or having only girl child and no son (8.55%), misunderstanding between family members (8.52%), ignorance of husband and in-laws (8.49%) and mistrust by husband or in-laws (5.68%) were identified as the salient reasons of domestic violence in both communities.

Despite this, the preference of the causes of domestic violence differed in accordance with the rural-urban residential settings. Thus, percent cases for the main causes of domestic violence were determined for rural and urban settings separately. Table 3.4 and 3.5 display hierarchy of the causes of domestic violence reported by participants are in the following order:

Table 3.4: Displays Main Causes of Domestic Violence in Rural Areas.

Sl. No.	*Causes*	*Frequency*	*Percent-ages(%)*
1.	Alcohol/chewing tobacco	20	28.17
2.	Lack of money	16	22.54
3.	Unemployment	14	19.72
4.	Conflict between wife and husband	12	16.90
5.	Differences in attitudes	11	15.49
6.	Dowry	10	14.08
7.	Ego problem with in-laws	10	14.08
8.	If she has done any work without permission	10	14.08
9.	Gambling	8	11.27
10.	Rude behaviour of family members	8	11.27
11.	Authoritarian behaviour of husband and in-laws	8	11.27
12.	Conflict with mother in-law and sister in-laws	14	19.72
13.	Extra marital affair	7	9.86
14.	Illiteracy	7	9.86
15.	High restrictions by husband and in-laws	4	5.63
16.	Misunderstanding between family members	3	4.23
17.	Interference of relatives and neighbours	3	4.23
18.	Mistrust	2	2.82
19.	No child (Infertility)	1	1.41

(ii) In Rural Community: The main causes of domestic violence in rural areas are displayed in preferential order in Table 3.5. The alcohol or tobacco (28.17%) is the main reason of domestic violence in rural families. The next orders of causes are: lack of money or poverty (22.54%), unemployment (19.72%), conflict between husband and wife (16.90%), differences in attitudes with husband or family members (15.49%), dowry (14.08%), ego problems with in laws (14.08%), no autonomy (14.08%), gambling (11.27%) mental harassment by family members (11.27%), dictatorship (authoritarian behaviour) of husband (11.27%), extra marital affair (9.86%), illiteracy (9.86%), dominance of in-laws (5.64%), interference of relatives and neighbours (4.23%), misunderstanding (4.23%), mistrust (2.82%) and infertility/only girl child and no son (1.41%) subsequently (Table 3.4).

(iii) In Urban Community: The salient reasons of domestic violence in preferential order are recorded in Table 3.5. In urban setting the conflict between husband-wife (30%) is the main cause of domestic violence. The order of other

Table 3.5: Displays Main Causes of Domestic Violence in Urban Areas.

Sl. No.	*Causes*	*Frequency*	*Percent-ages(%)*
1.	Conflict between wife and husband/in-laws	21	30
2.	Mental torture	14	20.0
3.	Dowry	8	11.43
4.	Less money, more expenditure	8	11.43
5.	Lack of money	7	10.0
6.	Alcohol/chewing tobacco	7	10.0
7.	Unemployment	6	8.57
8.	Children (No. of children/girl child but, no son)	5	7.14
9.	Illiteracy	5	7.14
10.	Stress	5	7.14
11.	Not completing work in time	5	7.14
12.	Mental and Physical torture for family property	5	7.14
13.	Mistrust provoked by others	5	7.14
14.	Excessive sexual behaviour	4	5.71
15.	Ego problem with husband and in-laws	4	5.71
16.	Giving no importance/attention to her feelings	4	5.71
17.	Extra marital affair (Female and male)	4	5.71
18.	Gambling	4	5.71
19.	Misunderstanding between family members	3	4.29
20.	Differences in views	3	4.29
21.	Authoritarian behaviour of husband and in-laws	3	4.29
22.	Depression	2	2.86
23.	Sexual harassment of daughter (by father)	2	2.86
24.	Mistrust	2	2.86
25.	Suppressing (her feelings/dominance)	2	2.86
26.	Sexual harassment by father-in law	1	1.43

causes of domestic violence are: Mental torture (sarcastic behaviour) (20%), dowry demands (11.43%), high expenditure (11.43%), lack of money (10%), alcohol addiction (10%), unemployment (8.57%), infertility or no son (7.14%), illiteracy (7.14%), family stress (7.14%), household chores to be completed on time (7.14%), high demand for family property (7.14%), mistrust provoked by others (7.14%), excessive demand of sexual behaviour (5.71%), ego clashes with husband and in-laws (5.71%), emotional neglect (5.71%), extra-marital affairs (5.71%), gambling (5.71%), misunderstanding among family members (4.29%), differences in views (4.29%), dictatorship (authoritarian behaviour) of husband and in- laws (4.29%), depression (2.86%) sexual harassment of daughter by husband (2.86%), mistrust (2.86%), and sexual harassment by father in-law (1.43) respectively. Results, thus, evinced that certain causes of domestic violence are common in both communities however, some reasons of domestic violence, are context specific.

II. Social Factors of Domestic Violence

The second objective of the study was to identify the social factors (socio-demographic characteristic of women, husband, family and environmental setting), which play detrimental role in the origin and sustenance of domestic violence.

The socio-economic status, caste and other social characteristics of perpetrators and abused victims were determined with the help of Personal Data Sheet (PDS). Scored data were analyzed in terms of Means & (weighted mean) SDs, Analysis of Variance (ANOVA), Correlations and Step-Wise Multiple Regression (SWMR) Analysis respectively. Results are displayed in Tables and Figures.

Domestic Violence in Relation to Socio-Demographic Characteristics—Obtained results evinced the role of social and demographic factors in the origin of domestic violence. These social factors were identified as major determinants of domestic violence. Results are reported in a nutshell.

A. Domestic Violence by the Women Characteristics

Certain socio-demographic characteristics of women like age, education and health status of women were found associated with domestic violence.

(a) Age—Results displayed in Table 3.6 and Fig.3.3 indicate a consistent pattern of age differences towards the incidence of domestic violence. Results indicate that women of middle age (45+) reported high abusing experiences than younger age women. Significant F-value [F(3,137) = 6.45, P< .000] for economic abuse indicates that economic abuse was found higher in middle age women (M = 22.33) than those of younger women (M = 12.11).

Table 3.6: Shows Means & Weighted Means, SDs and F-'values' of various forms of domestic violence in different age groups of females.

Type of D.V. (Abuses) / Age Group		Physical Abuse	Sexual Abuse	Psycho-logical Abuse	Economic Abuse	Abuse as a whole
Below 25 Yrs.						
	Mean	37.32	17.63	76.37	12.11	143.21
	WM	149.28	211.56	229.11	145.32	735.27
	SD	10.44	5.33	25.96	3.45	40.64
25-35 Yrs.						
	Mean	39.75	16.6	80.96	15.34	152.51
	WM	159	199.2	242.88	184.08	785.16
	SD	14.27	5.98	22.31	6.45	42.51
35-45 Yrs.						
	Mean	44.74	17.32	83.03	19.65	164.84
	WM	178.96	207.84	249.09	235.8	871.69
	SD	17.37	6.87	20.57	9.34	47.96
Above 45 Yrs.						
	Mean	47.33	17.33	90.50	22.33	177.50
	WM	189.32	207.96	270	267.96	935.24
	SD	20.65	7.50	28.74	10.69	62.80
	F-'Values'	1.58	0.13	0.67	6.45**	1.49

** P< .01

* P< .05

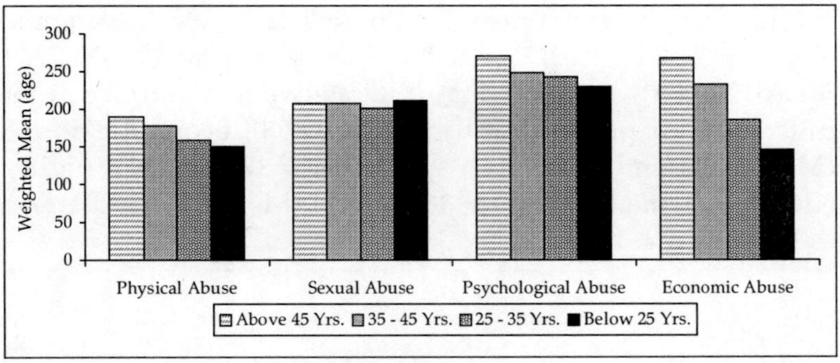

Fig. 3.3: Displays domestic violence (abuses) as a function of different age group of females.

(b) Education—Results (Table 3.7 and Figure 3.4) reveal that various forms of domestic violence differed significantly across different education level of women. The significant

Table 3.7: Displays Means & Weighted Means, SDs and F-'values' of various forms of domestic violence across different education level of females.

Education Level	*Type of D.V. (Abuses)*	*Physical Abuse*	*Sexual Abuse*	*Psycho-logical Abuse*	*Economic Abuse*	*Abuse as a whole*
Illiterate	**Mean**	**47.98**	**17.69**	**87.21**	**20.02**	**173.10**
	WM	**191.92**	**212.28**	**261.63**	**240.24**	**906.07**
	SD	**18.20**	**6.64**	**24.60**	**8.99**	**52.77**
0-5	**Mean**	**38.26**	**17.70**	**79.13**	**14.57**	**148.17**
	WM	**153.04**	**212.40**	**237.39**	**174.84**	**777.67**
	SD	**10.78**	**6.04**	**18.58**	**5.56**	**34.08**
6-12	**Mean**	**36.00**	**16.08**	**77.83**	**13.75**	**143.58**
	WM	**144.00**	**192.96**	**233.49**	**165.00**	**735.45**
	SD	**10.86**	**5.56**	**21.56**	**5.61**	**35.90**
Above 12	**Mean**	**36.57**	**17.00**	**74.86**	**13.29**	**141.71**
	WM	**146.28**	**204.00**	**224.58**	**159.48**	**734.34**
	SD	**11.04**	**6.35**	**22.46**	**4.01**	**37.99**
	F-'Values'	**7.22****	**.66**	**2.28**	**8.63****	**4.96****

** P< .01

* P< .05

F-values of physical abuse [F(3,137) = 7.22 P< .001], economic abuse [F(3,137) = 8.63, P< .001] and abuse as a whole [F(3,137) = 4.96, P< .001] indicates that illiterate women suffered from high level of physical abuse (M = 47.98), economic abuse (M = 20.02) and abuse as a whole (M = 173.10) than highly educated women[(M(Phy) = 36.57, (eco) (M = 13.29) and abuse as whole (M = 141.71)].

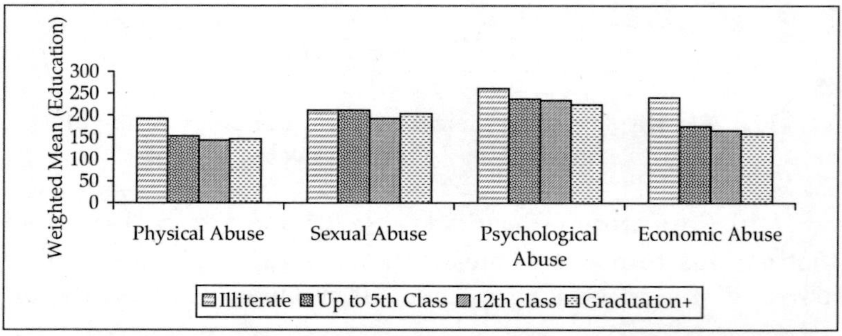

Fig. 3.4: Displays domestic violence (abuses) as a function of different education level of females.

(c) Health Status—As is apparent from Table 3.8 and Fig. 3.5, health status of the women was also found as an important

Table 3.8: Shows Means & Weighted Means, SDs and F-'values' of various forms of domestic violence in different health status of females

Health Status	*Type of D.V. (Abuses)*	*Physical Abuse*	*Sexual Abuse*	*Psycho-logical Abuse*	*Economic Abuse*	*Abuse as a whole*
Sick	**Mean**	**44.72**	**18.66**	**91.47**	**17.78**	**171.56**
	WM	**178.88**	**223.92**	**274.41**	**213.36**	**890.57**
	SD	**16.07**	**5.34**	**20.81**	**8.70**	**49.70**
Normal	**Mean**	**43.37**	**17.21**	**82.69**	**17.17**	**160.52**
	WM	**173.48**	**206.52**	**248.07**	**206.04**	**834.11**
	SD	**16.82**	**5.63**	**23.03**	**7.77**	**46.56**
Good	**Mean**	**32.87**	**15.32**	**69.79**	**12.87**	**130.84**
	WM	**131.48**	**183.84**	**209.37**	**154.44**	**679.84**
	SD	**6.66**	**5.56**	**18.62**	**4.45**	**27.04**
	F-'Values'	**8.26****	**2.73***	**9.23****	**5.37****	**9.28****

** P< .01
* P< .05

contributing factor of domestic violence. The significant F-values of Physical abuse [F(3,137) = 8.26, P< .000], psychological abuse [F(3, 137) = 9.23, P< .000], economic abuse [F(3,137) = 5.37, P< .01] and (abuse) as a whole [F(3, 137) = 9.28, P< .000] indicate that the women with poor health status reported to be high victims of physical abuse (M = 44.72), psychological abuse (M = 91.47), economic abuse (M = 17.78) and abuse as a whole (M = 171.56) than women having normal and good health status respectively.

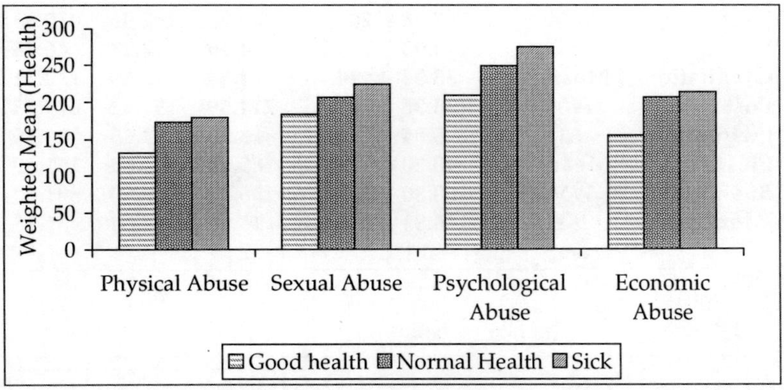

Fig. 3.5.: Displays domestic violence (abuses) in relation to different health status of females

B. Husband's Characteristics

Certain husband's characteristics, i.e., education, occupation and income were found associated with domestic violence. The findings are interpreted in the following manner:

(a) Education: Results (Table 3.9 and Fig. 3.6) denote that husband's education also influenced the level of domestic violence. The significant F-values for physical abuse [F(3,137) = 4.21, P< .000], sexual abuse [F(3,137) = 2.77, P< .05], psychological abuse [F(3,137) = 2.95, P< .05], economic abuse [F(3,137) = 4.94, P< .000] and abuse as a whole [F(3,137) = 4.60, P< .000] indicate that illiterate or low educated husbands were reported highly abusive than highly educated counterparts (see Table 3.9 and Fig. 3.6).

Table 3.9: Shows Means & Weighted Means, SDs and F-'values' of various forms of domestic violence across different education lavel of husband

Husband's Education	*Type of D.V. (Abuses)*	*Physical Abuse*	*Sexual Abuse*	*Psycho-logical Abuse*	*Economic Abuse*	*Abuse as a whole*
0-5	**Mean**	**45.20**	**18.85**	**86.63**	**19.15**	**169.73**
	WM	**180.82**	**226.20**	**259.89**	**229.80**	**896.69**
	SD	**16.25**	**6.91**	**22.33**	**8.77**	**47.16**
6-12	**Mean**	**41.87**	**16.97**	**82.25**	**16.08**	**157.22**
	WM	**167.48**	**203.64**	**246.75**	**192.96**	**810.83**
	SD	**16.03**	**5.74**	**24.16**	**7.27**	**46.78**
Graduation/ Post graduation	**Mean**	**33.34**	**14.78**	**71.53**	**12.66**	**132.41**
	WM	**133.36**	**177.36**	**214.59**	**151.92**	**677.23**
	SD	**8.04**	**5.13**	**18.56**	**4.63**	**28.59**
Ph.D./ Business Education	**Mean**	**40.20**	**17.20**	**85.40**	**14.80**	**151.60**
	WM	**160.80**	**206.4**	**256.20**	**177.60**	**801.00**
	SD	**6.83**	**6.38**	**14.50**	**4.60**	**31.16**
	F-'Values'	**4.21****	**2.77***	**2.95***	**4.94****	**4.60****

** P< .01
* P< .05

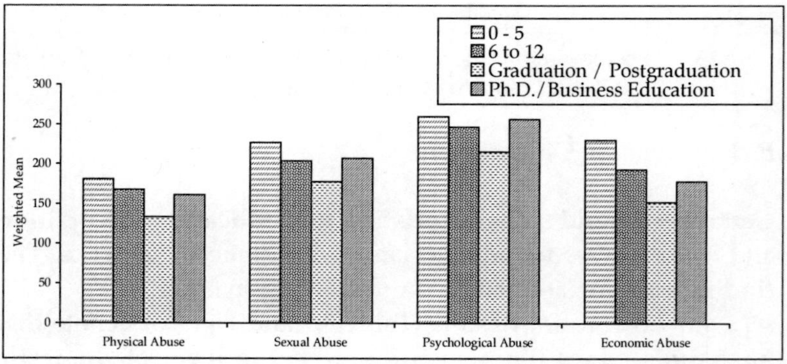

Fig. 3.6: Shows domestic violence (abuses) in relation to different

(b) Occupation of Husband—Results displayed in Table 3.10 and Fig. 3.7 reveal that occupation of husband also predicted the levels of domestic violence. The significant F-values for psychological abuse [F(3, 137) = 2.90, P< .05], economic abuse [F(3, 137) = 5.16, P< .01] and abuse as a whole [F(3, 137) = 3.10, P< .05] indicate that domestic violence differed

across occupational characteristics of the husband/family. Husbands of labour class were found more abusive (psy. abuse, eco abuse and abuse as a whole) than other occupational group (See Table 3.1 and Fig. 3.7)

Table 3.10: Shows Means & Weighted Means, SDs and F-'values' of various forms of domestic violence across different occupational characteristics of husband

Husband's Occupation	*Type of D.V. (Abuses)*	*Physical Abuse*	*Sexual Abuse*	*Psycho-logical Abuse*	*Economic Abuse*	*Abuse as a whole*
Labour	**Mean**	**44.50**	**17.50**	**88.40**	**21.15**	**171.55**
	WM	**178**	**210**	**265.2**	**253.8**	**907**
	SD	**15.83**	**6.20**	**23.91**	**8.44**	**46.28**
Farmer	**Mean**	**33.00**	**15.21**	**66.50**	**11.64**	**126.07**
	WM	**132**	**182.52**	**199.5**	**139.68**	**653.7**
	SD	**6.56**	**4.59**	**15.01**	**2.44**	**21.63**
Business	**Mean**	**41.34**	**17.39**	**82.98**	**15.92**	**157.73**
	WM	**165.36**	**208**	**248.94**	**191.04**	**814.02**
	SD	**15.51**	**6.05**	**23.17**	**7.62**	**45.26**
Service	**Mean**	**41.00**	**16.92**	**80.31**	**15.67**	**153.27**
	WM	**164**	**203.04**	**240.93**	**188.04**	**796.02**
	SD	**15.24**	**6.59**	**21.94**	**6.95**	**45.22**
	F-'Values'	**1.73**	**.52**	**2.90***	**5.16****	**3.10***

** P< .01
* P< .05

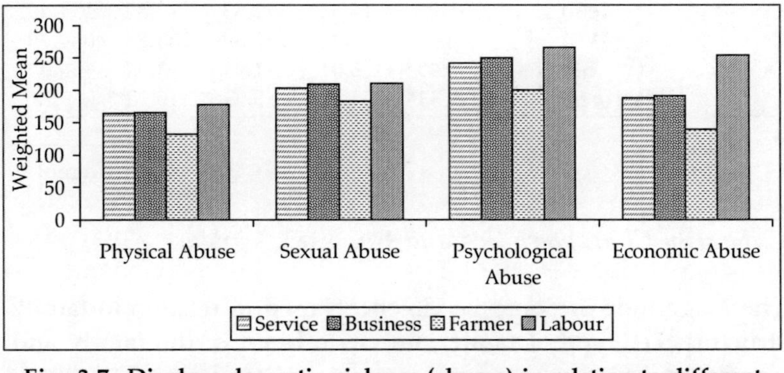

Fig. 3.7: Displays domestic violence (abuses) in relation to different occupational characteristics of husband

(c) Income—Results (Table 3.11 and Fig. 3.8) further denote that husband's income level also influenced the level of domestic violence (women abuses). The significant F-values for physical abuse [F(3, 137) = 9.53, P< .000], sexual abuse [F(3, 137) = 4.82, P< .01], psychological abuse [F(3, 137) = 5.03, P< .01], economic abuse [F(3, 137) = 10.20, P< .000] and abuse as a whole [F(3, 137) = 9.28, P< .000] indicate that husband of low income (below 5000) group reported to be high abusive as compared to middle and high income group (see Table 3.11 and Fig 3.8).

Table 3.11: Displays Means & Weighted Means, SDs and F-'values' of various forms of domestic violence in different income level of husband

Type of D.V. (Abuses) / *Husband's Income*	*Physical Abuse*	*Sexual Abuse*	*Psycho-logical Abuse*	*Economic Abuse*	*Abuse as a whole*
Below Rs. 5000/-					
Mean	**46.60**	**18.47**	**87.16**	**90.08**	**171.24**
WM	**186.4**	**221.64**	**261.48**	**270.24**	**939.76**
SD	**17.25**	**5.87**	**22.89**	**9.10**	**48.17**
Rs. 5000-10,000/-					
Mean	**37.33**	**16.93**	**79.56**	**14.62**	**148.51**
WM	**149.32**	**203.16**	**238.68**	**175.44**	**766.6**
SD	**12.10**	**6.02**	**20.85**	**5.61**	**37.52**
Above Rs. 10,000/-					
Mean	**35.00**	**14.53**	**72.53**	**12.82**	**134.09**
WM	**140**	**174.36**	**217.59**	**153.84**	**684.79**
SD	**9.47**	**6.01**	**21.94**	**3.57**	**36.04**
F-'Values'	**9.53****	**4.82****	**5.03****	**10.20****	**9.28****

** P< .01
* P< .05

C. Family Characteristics and Domestic Violence

The magnitude of domestic violence varied in relation to family structure, i.e., type of family, no. of children in the family and size of family.

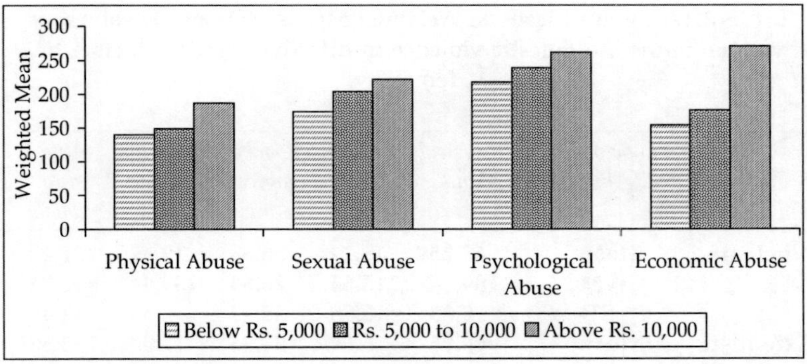

Fig. 3.8: Displays domestic violence (abuses) in relation to different income level of husband

(a) Family Structure—Findings evinced that women belonging to joint, extended and nuclear families varied significantly on domestic violence. Significant F-value for abuse as whole [F(3,137) = 9.27, P< .000] indicates that women of nuclear families were found high victims of D. V. than females of extended (M = 158.88) and joint families (M = 138.97). Similarly, significant F-values for physical abuse [F(3,137) = 12.34, P< .000], psychological abuse [F(3, 137) = 4.52, P< .01], economic abuse [F(3,137) = 11.27, P< .000] reveals that various forms of abuses were found higher in nuclear families.

(b) Family Size: Findings evinced (Table 3.13 and Fig. 3.10) that women belonging to various no. of family members varied significantly on domestic violence. Women belonging to less than five members of family were found high victims of domestic violence than females of greater number of family members. Significant F-values for physical abuse [F(3,137) = 5.54, P< .000], sexual abuse [F(3,137) = 2.95, P< .05], psychological abuse [F(3,137) = 4.05, P< .05], economic abuse [F(3,137) = 5.75, P< .000] and abuse as a whole [F(3,137) = 6.73, P<.000] suggest that various forms of abuses were found higher in small family size (below 5) then medium and big size families. This result also supports that D.V is found at high rate in nuclear families than extended or joint family patterns.

Table 3.12: Shows Means & Weighted Means, SDs and F-'values' of various forms of domestic violence in different family structure of females.

Type of Family	*Type of D.V. (Abuses)*	*Physical Abuse*	*Sexual Abuse*	*Psycho-logical Abuse*	*Economic Abuse*	*Abuse as a whole*
Nuclear	**Mean**	47.25	18.22	86.88	19.12	171.40
	WM	189	218.64	26.64	229.44	897.72
	SD	18.03	6.68	25.12	8.55	52.45
Extended	**Mean**	40.94	16.69	84.25	17.00	158.88
	WM	163.76	200.28	252.75	204	820.79
	SD	14.67	7.16	23.97	9.40	42.10
Joint	**Mean**	34.91	16.02	75.22	13.20	138.97
	WM	139.64	192.24	225.66	158.4	755.94
	SD	8.06	5.11	18.37	4.19	29.67
	F-'Values'	12.34**	2.08	4.52*	11.27**	9.27**

** P< .01
* P< .05

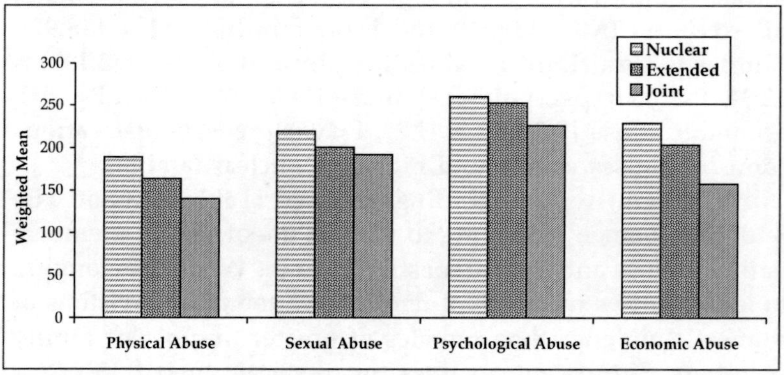

Fig. 3.9: Displays domestic violence (abuses) in relation to different family structure of females

Table 3.13: Shows Means & Weighted Means, SDs and F-'values' of various forms of domestic violence across different family size of females.

Family Size	*Type of D.V. (Abuses)*	*Physical Abuse*	*Sexual Abuse*	*Psycho-logical Abuse*	*Economic Abuse*	*Abuse as a whole*
Below 5	**Mean**	46.71	19.67	88.29	18.96	173.46
	WM	183.64	231.6	139.56	225.96	780.76
	SD	17.91	8.00	22.01	8.61	50.12
5-10	**Mean**	41.94	16.71	82.91	16.94	158.04
	WM	167.76	200.52	248.73	203.28	820.29
	SD	15.35	6.00	23.92	7.95	47.06
Above 10	**Mean**	34.68	16	72.92	12.62	136.57
	WM	138.72	192	218.76	151.44	700.92
	SD	9.15	4.44	17.91	3.02	26.49
	F-'Values'	5.54**	2.95*	4.05*	5.75**	6.73**

** P< .01
* P< .05

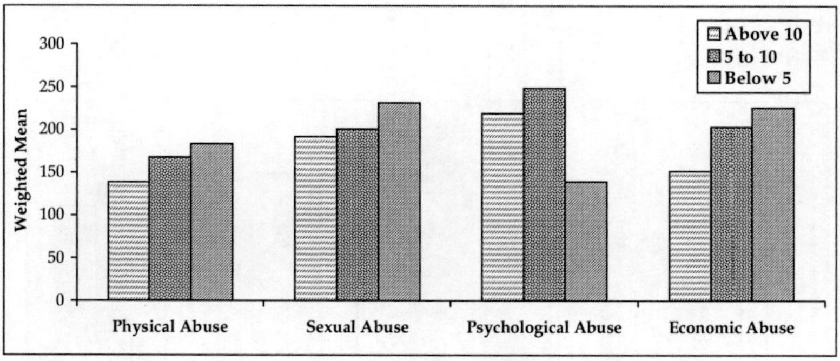

Fig. 3.10: Displays domestic violence (abuses) in relation to different family size of females

(c) No. of Children—Table 3.14 and Fig. 3.11 show that the women having more daughters were found to be high victims of abuse [(abuse as a whole) (F(3, 137)= 3.04, P< .05), economic abuse (F(3, 137)= 4.95, P< .01)] than those having only one or no girl child [abuse as a whole (M = 18.32) and (M(Eco) = 165.15)] respectively.

Table 3.14: Displays Means & Weighted Means, SDs and F-'values' of various forms of domestic violence in case of females with different No. of children

No. of Children \ Type of D.V. (Abuses)		Physical Abuse	Sexual Abuse	Psycho-logical Abuse	Economic Abuse	Abuse as a whole
0 (No Child)	Mean	35.67	14.25	71.83	13.08	134.25
	WM	142.68	171	215.49	156.96	686.13
	SD	11.02	6.15	23.77	4.94	41.52
1-2	Mean	36.47	17.10	77.80	13.59	144.88
	WM	145.88	205.2	233.4	163.08	747.56
	SD	8.79	5.83	19.44	4.33	28.95
3-5	Mean	44.08	17.48	85.12	18.32	165.15
	WM	176.32	209.76	255.36	219.84	861.28
	SD	17.32	6.35	23.33	8.65	49.84
Above 6	Mean	45.36	17.00	82.71	17.50	160.64
	WM	181.44	204	248.13	210	843.57
	SD	18.71	5.88	26.97	9.10	56.40
	F-'Values'	3.51	.95	1.76	4.95**	3.04*

** P< .01
* P< .05

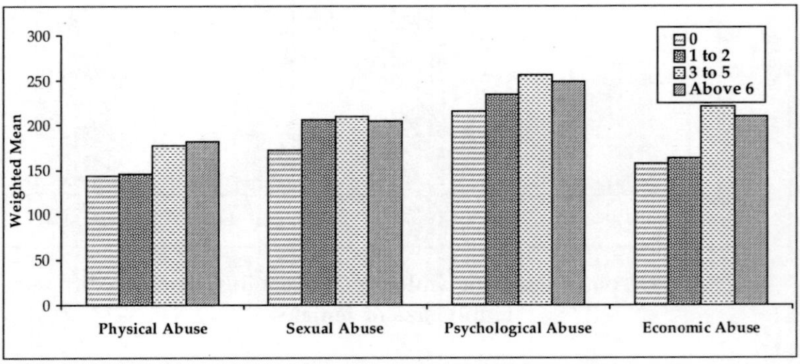

Fig. 3.11: Displays domestic violence (abuses) in relation to females with different number of children

Similarly, significant F-value [F(3, 137) = 3.51, P< .01] for physical abuse indicates that physical abuse was found higher in families having greater no. of girl child (M = 45.36) than their comparison groups (M = 35.67) respectively.

D. Social Factors

Certain social characteristics i.e., socio-economic status (SES), caste and community also influenced the various forms of domestic violence.

(a) Socio-Economic Status (SES)—Table 3.15 and Fig. 3.12 denote that socio-economic status also contributed to domestic violence. The women belonging to low SES reported high victims of abuses. The significant F-values of physical abuse [F(3, 137) = 18.24, P< .000], sexual abuse [F(3, 137) = 7.20, P< .01], psychological abuse [F(3, 137) = 12.54, P< .000], economic abuse [F(3, 137) = 21.77, P< .000] and abuse as a whole [F(3, 137) = 19.86; P< .000] indicate that women belonging to low SES reported high incidences of physical abuse, sexual abuse, psychological abuse, economic abuse and abuse as a whole than Middle and High S.E.S females. (Table 3.15).

Table 3.15: Shows Means & Weighted Means, SDs and F-'values' of various forms of domestic violence across different socio-economic status of females.

Socio-economic Status	*Type of D.V. (Abuses)*	*Physical Abuse*	*Sexual Abuse*	*Psycho-logical Abuse*	*Economic Abuse*	*Abuse as a whole*
Low	**Mean**	49.73	19.43	90.13	20.75	180.55
	WM	198.92	233.16	272.19	249	953.27
	SD	17.71	5.92	22.94	8.79	48.47
Middle	**Mean**	37.35	16.23	81.90	14.94	150.63
	WM	149.4	194.76	245.7	179.28	769.14
	SD	11.70	5.92	20.91	6.16	37.37
High	**Mean**	34.05	15.02	68.86	11.95	129.07
	WM	136.2	180.24	206.58	143.4	666.42
	SD	8.06	5.71	18.44	2.85	28.74
	F-'Values'	18.24**	7.20**	12.54*	21.77**	19.86**

** P< .01
* P< .05

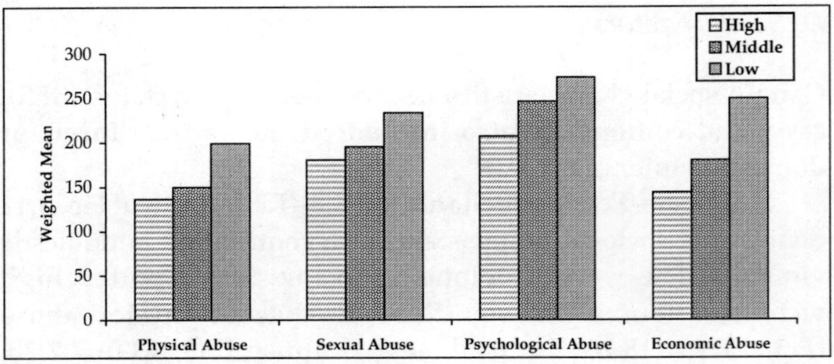

Fig. 3.12: Displays domestic violence (abuses) as a function of different socio-economic status of females

(b) Caste—Results (Table 3.16 and Fig. 3.13) revealed that domestic violence differed significantly across different caste compositions. The significant F-values for physical abuse [F(3, 137) = 10.24, P< .000], sexual abuse [F(3, 137) = 7.96, P< .01], economic abuse [F(3, 137) = 10.56, P< .000] and abuse as a whole [F(3, 137) = 7.39, P< .001] indicate that schedule caste women were found to be very high victims of physical abuse, sexual abuse, economic abuse and abuse as a whole than OBC women and minimum abuse was reported by high caste women (Table 3.16).

Table 3.16: Shows Means & Weighted Means, SDs and F-'values' of various forms of domestic violence across different caste of females.

Caste	*Type of D.V. (Abuses)*	*Physical Abuse*	*Sexual Abuse*	*Psycho-logical Abuse*	*Economic Abuse*	*Abuse as a whole*
SC	Mean	49.64	21.79	84.21	20.36	176.00
	WM	198.56	261.48	252.63	254.32	956.99
	SD	20.15	5.44	23.69	11.21	57.17
OBC	Mean	46.49	18.22	86.35	19.16	117.35
	WM	185.96	218.64	259.05	229.92	903.57
	SD	15.29	5.87	22.31	7.80	43.93
General	Mean	36.49	15.63	78.07	13.92	143.69
	WM	145.96	187.56	234.21	166.8	734.53
	SD	12.11	5.87	22.38	5.62	39.40
	F-'Values'	10.24**	7.96**	2.07	10.56**	7.39**

** P< .01

* P< .05

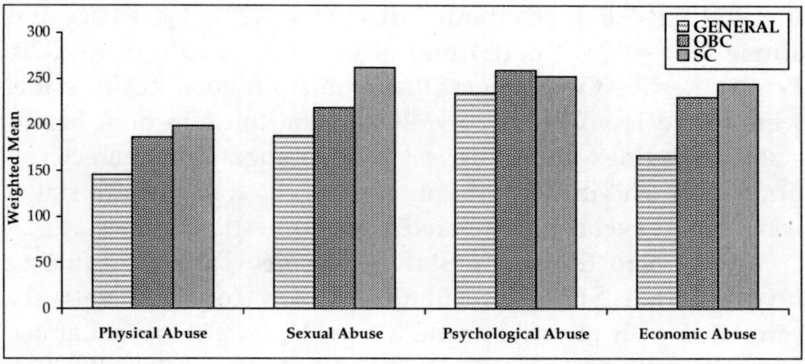

Fig. 3.13: Displays domestic violence (abuses) as a function of different caste of females

Correlational Analysis

In order to determine the linkages between demographic characteristic and domestic violence, correlations were computed. Results are displayed in Table 3.17.

(A) Relationship between various demographic factors and domestic violence

1. Women's Characteristics

(i) Age—Correlations displayed in Table 3.17 denote positive relationship between women's age and various forms of abuses viz., physical abuse ($r = .180$, $P< .05$), economic abuse ($r = .35$, $P< .01$) and abuse as a whole ($r = .18$ $P< .05$), which suggests that the levels of abuse increased with increasing the age of women.

(ii) Education—Results further revealed that education was found to be inversely proportional with physical abuse ($r = -.34$, $P< .01$), psychological abuse ($r = -.20$ $P< .05$), and economic abuse ($r = -.37$, $P< .01$). Results thus, suggest that with increasing the education level of women, degree of domestic violence decreased.

(iii) Health Status—Correlations, further denote that women's health status was found to be negatively related with physical abuse ($r = -.289$, $P< .01$), psychological abuse

(r = -.340, P< .01), economic abuse (r = –.239, P< .01) sexual abuse (r = –.194, P<. 05) and abuse as a whole (r = –.328, P< .01). Results thus, suggest that women in good health status were found low victims of violence than those in poor health status. Findings, thus, suggest that demographic characteristics of women viz. age, education, SES, caste and health status were found exclusively related with domestic violence.

(iv) Socio Economic Status—Results (Table 3.17) further revealed that SES of respondents was found negatively correlated with physical abuse (r = –.434, P< .01), sexual abuse (r = –.297, P< .01), psychological abuse (r = –.390, P< .01), economic abuse (r = –.482, P< .01) and abuse as a whole (r = -.471, P< .01). Findings, thus suggest that with increasing the socio-economic status of women, the extent of abuses decreased.

Table 3.17 : Shows relationship between demographic variables and various forms of domestic violence.

Demographic Variables \ *Domestic Violence*	*Physical Abuse*	*Sexual Abuse*	*Psycho-logical Abuse*	*Economic Abuse*	*Abuse as a whole*
Woman (victim)'s					
Age	.180*	.002	.12	.35**	.18*
Education	-.34**	-.09	-.20*	-.37**	-.29
Health Status	-.289**	-.194*	-.340**	-.239**	-.328**
Socio-economic Status	-.434**	-.297**	-.390**	-.482**	-.471**
Caste	-.347**	-.320**	-.143	-.351**	-.296**
Husband's: Education	-.249**	-.208*	-.190*	-.290**	-.267**
Occupation	-.01	.001	-.04	-.15	-.05
Income	-.33**	-.25**	-.26**	-.35**	-.34**
Family Structure	-.390**	-.170*	.244**	-.373**	-.343**
Family Size	.270**	.181*	.230**	.289**	.275**
No. of Children	.24	.09	.17*	.26**	.22**

** P< .01, *P< .05, N = 140

(v) Caste—Correlations between caste and domestic violence were also computed. Results revealed that caste of women was found negatively related with physical abuse

(r= –.347, P< .01), sexual abuse (r = –.320, P< .01), economic abuse (r = –.351, P< .01) and abuse as a whole (r = –.296, P< .01). Results, thus suggest that with increasing caste level of respondents, domestic violence decreased.

B. Husband Characteristics

(i) Husband's Education—Correlation results further revealed that husband's education was found inversely related with physical abuse (r = –.249, P<.01), sexual abuse (r = –.208, P< .05), psychological abuse (r= –.190, P< .05), economic abuse (r = –.290, P< .01) and abuse as a whole (r = –.267, P< .01). Results thus, suggest that with increasing the education level of husband, the degree of domestic violence decreased.

(ii) Husband's Occupation—Correlations indicate that husband's occupation was found negatively related with economic abuse (r= –.15) and abuse as a whole (r= –.054). Results, thus, indicate that permanently employed husbands were found less abusive than temporary and labour class husbands.

(iii) Income—Correlation results (Table 3.17) further reveal that income was found negatively correlated with physical abuse (r= –.33, P< .01), sexual abuse (r = –.253, P< .01), psychological abuse (r = –.26, P< .01), economic abuse (r= –.349, P< .01) and abuse as a whole (r = –.34, P< .01). Findings, thus, suggest that the extent of various forms of domestic violence decreased with increasing income level of the family.

C. Family Characteristics

(i) Family Structure—Correlation between family structure and domestic violence was also calculated. As Table 3.17 shows that type of family was found to be negatively related with physical abuse (r = –.390, P< .01), psychological abuse (r = –.244 P< .01), sexual abuse (r = –.170, P< .05), economic abuse (r= –.373, P< .01) and abuse as a whole (r = –.343, P< .05). The relationship evinces that the level of violence was found higher in nuclear families than joint and extended families.

(ii) Family Size: Table 3.17 shows that family size was found to be positively related with physical abuse (r = .270, P< .01), sexual abuse (r = .181, P< .05), psychological abuse (r= .230, P< .01), economic abuse (r = .289, P< .01) and abuse as a whole (r= .275, P< .01). Results thus, suggest that increasing the no. of family members, violence against women, increased.

(iii) No. of Children: Correlation results indicate that no. of children was found positively related with psychological abuse (r = .17, P< .05), economic abuse (r = .26, P< .05) and abuse as a whole (r = .22, P< .01). Findings, thus, suggest that the various forms of domestic violence increased with increasing the no. of children.

III. Psychological Dynamics of Domestic Violence

Third objective of the study was to investigate the role of psychological variable i.e., marital conflict, life stress and women empowerment in domestic violence. In order to determine the influence of these psychological factors on incidence of Domestic Violence, the responses obtained on various measures were scored and treated statistically. Results are displayed in Tables and Figures and interpreted below:

1. The Role of Marital Conflict in Domestic Violence—The level of marital conflict was determined on the basis of scores obtained on Marital Conflict Scale. Respondents were divided into high and low conflict groups on the basis of median score (Mdn = 85). Furthermore, to ascertain the significant influence of marital conflict on domestic violence, comparative analysis (t-test) was done. Results are displayed in Table 3.18 and Fig 3.14 respectively.

It is apparent from the result that marital conflict caused high level of domestic violence [t (139) = 7.86, P< .000]. Results suggest that women who reported high level of conflict with husband, were found highly abused than the females confronting with low level of marital conflict. Similarly, the impact of marital conflict was also identified on the various forms of abuses. The significant difference between high and low conflict groups were also found on physical abuse [t (139) = 6.64, P< .000], sexual abuse [t (139) = 4.13, P< .000] and economic abuse [t (139) = 6.24, P< .000]. Results evinced that women with high level of conflict were found high victims of various forms of abuses [(M Phy. abuse = (48), Sex. abuse = (19), Psy. abuse = (92.49), Eco. abuse = (19.57) and abuse as a whole = (179.19)] than their low conflict counterparts [M(Phy.) = (33.38), psy. = (69.43), sex = (14.97), eco. = (12.58) and abuse as a whole = (129.81)] respectively.

Table 3.18: Means, SDs and 't'–values for various forms of domestic violence (abuses) between high and low conflict groups

Dimensions of domestic violence	*High Conflict*		*Low Conflict*		*t*
	Mean	*SD*	*Mean*	*SD*	
Physical Abuse	48.00	16.70	33.38	7.66	6.64**
Sexual Abuse	19.00	6.82	14.97	4.47	4.13**
Psychological Abuse	92.49	20.31	69.43	18.72	7.00**
Economic Abuse	19.57	8.57	12.58	3.71	6.24**
Abuse as a whole	179.19	44.50	129.81	27.91	7.86**

** P<.01,* P<.05

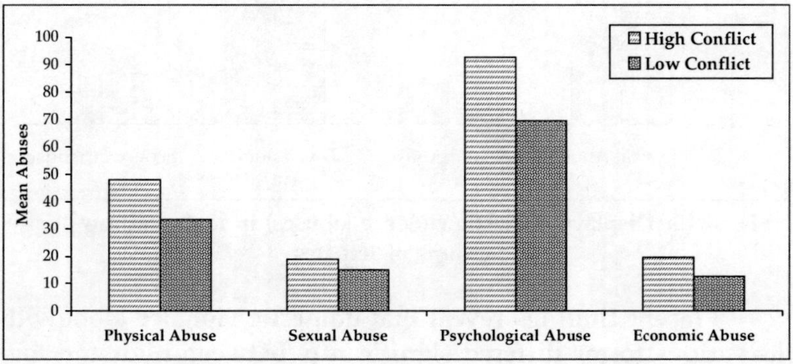

Fig. 3.14: Displays domestic violence (abuses) in high and low conflict groups of females

2. The Influence of Stress on Domestic Violence—The level of stress was determined on the basis of scores obtained on Life Stress Scale. Respondents were divided into high and low stressed groups on the basis of median score (Mdn = 49). Furthermore, to ascertain the influence of stress on domestic violence, Mean, SD and t-tests were computed for responses

given on D.V. Checklist. Results are displayed in Table 3.19 and Fig 3.15.

Table 3.19: Means, SDs and 't'–values for various forms of domestic violence (abuses) between high and low stress group of females.

Dimesions of Domestic Violence Variable	*High Stress*		*Low Stress*		*t*
	Mean	*SD*	*Mean*	*SD*	
Physical Abuse	47.03	17.38	33.82	6.61	5.81**
Sexual Abuse	18.35	6.70	15.53	5.01	2.80**
Psychological Abuse	91.25	21.63	69.79	18.01	6.36**
Economic Abuse	19.28	8.56	12.59	3.66	5.89**
Abuse as a whole	175.64	47.12	131.61	26.92	6.69**

** P<.01,* P<.05

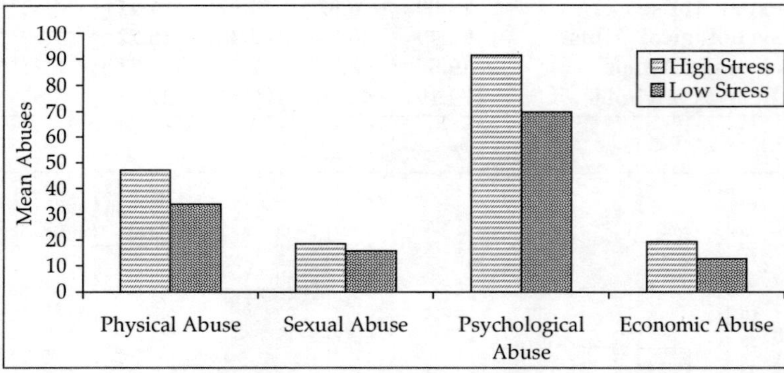

Fig. 3.15: Displays domestic violence (abuses) in high and low stress groups of females

Present findings reveal that domestic violence alongwith its various forms differed significantly between high and low stressed groups. The significant t-value on abuse as a whole [t (139) = 6.69, P< .000] indicates that women who had high feeling of stress reported high victims of abuse (M = 175.64.) than the women having low feeling of stress (M = 131.61). Similarly, the significant t-values for physical abuse [t (139) = 5.81, P< .000], sexual abuse [t (139) = 2.80, P< .000], psychological abuse [t (139) = 6.36, P< .000] and economic abuse [t (139) = 5.89, P< .000], reveal that the women with high level of stress were also found high victims of physical abuse

(M = 47.03), sexual abuse (M = 18.35), psychological abuse (M = 91.25), economic abuse (M= 19.28) and abuse as a whole (M = 175.64), than those of low conflict group [M(Phy.) = 33.82, M(Sex.) = 15.53, M(psy.) = 69.79, M(eco.) = 12.59 and M (abuse as a whole) = 131.61]. Results thus, evince that high level of life stress causes high incidence rate of domestic violence.

(3) The Role of Women Empowerment in Domestic Violence—The responses obtained on Women Empowerment Questionnaire were scored according to defined rules. Median score (Mdn = 77) was determined and females were divided into high and low empowered groups. Further, Means, SDs and t-values were computed for various forms of domestic violence. Results are displayed in Table 3.20 and Fig. 3.16.

Table 3.20: Means, SDs and 't'—values for various forms of domestic violence (abuses) between high and low empowered groups.

Dimensions of Domestic Violence	*High Empowered*		*Low Empowered*		*t*
	Mean	*SD*	*Mean*	*SD*	
Physical Abuse	35.69	10.30	46.22	17.10	4.45**
Sexual Abuse	15.22	5.17	18.91	6.47	3.75**
Psychological Abuse	73.39	19.29	89.36	23.15	4.46**
Economic Abuse	13.57	5.28	18.84	8.50	4.44**
Abuse as a whole	137.35	32.08	173.48	48.57	5.23**

** P<.01,* P<.05

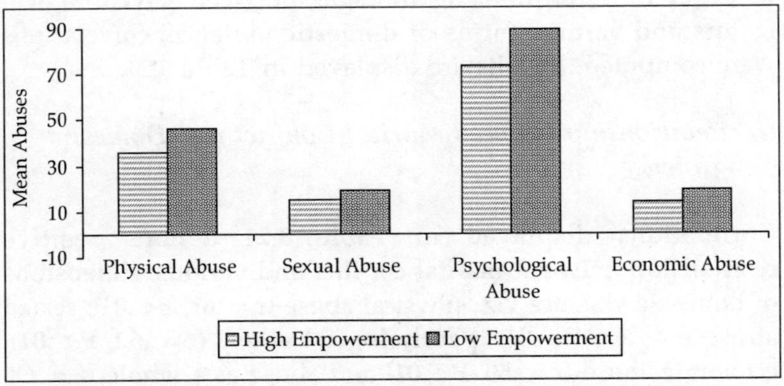

Fig. 3.16: Displays domestic violence (abuses) in high and low empowered groups of females

It is clear from the Table 3.20 and Fig. 3.16 that domestic violence varied across low empowered and high empowered groups [t (139) = 5.23, P< .000], which suggests that high empowered women were found less abused than low empowered women. Similarly, the significant differences between high and low empowered groups were found on physical abuse [t (139)= 4.45, P< .000], sexual abuse [t(139) = 3.75, P< .000], psychological abuse [t (139) = 4.46, P< .000] and economic abuse [t (139) = 4.44, P< .000]. Result reveals that the women with high level of empowerment were found low victims of physical abuse (M = 35.69), sexual abuse (M = 15.22), psychological abuse (M = 73.39), economic abuse (M = 13.57) and abuse as a whole (M = 137.35) than those of de empowered group [M(Phy.) = 46.22, (Sex.) = 18.91, (Psy.) = 89.36, (eco.) = 18.84 and [abuse as a whole) = 173.48], who were identified victims of various forms of abuses.

Results thus, evince that women having high level of marital conflict and high feeling of stress were also found high victims of domestic violence than their low comparison groups. Contrary to this, high empowered women reported low level of domestic violence than de empowered women.

The Relationship between Psychological Factors and Domestic Violence

In order to determine the linkages between psychological factors and various forms of domestic violence, correlations were computed. Results are displayed in Table 3.21.

(i) Relationship between Marital Conflict and Domestic Violence

Correlations displayed in Table 3.21 denote positive relationship between marital conflict and various dimensions of domestic violence viz., physical abuse (r = .61, P< .01), sexual abuse (r = .43, P< .01), psychological abuse (r = .62, P< .01), economic abuse (r = .59, P< .01) and abuse as a whole (r = .68, P< .01). Correlation results thus, suggest that the degree of domestic violence increased with increasing the level of marital conflict in the family.

(ii) Relationship between Stress and Domestic Violence

Correlations were computed between stress and various forms of domestic violence. Results (Table 3.21) revealed that stress was found to be positively related with physical abuse (r = .53, P< .01), sexual abuse (r = .35 P< .01), psychological abuse (r = .55, P< .01), economic abuse (r = .54, P< .01) and abuse as a whole (r = .60, P< .01). Results thus, indicate that with increasing level of stress, the intensity of domestic violence also increased.

(iii) Relationship between Women Empowerment and Domestic Violence

Correlation results (Table 3.21) further revealed that women empowerment was found to be negatively related with domestic violence. Empowerment was found inversely related with physical abuse (r= –.32, P< .01), sexual abuse (r = –.29, P< .01), psychological abuse (r =-.42, P< .01), economic abuse (r = –.30, P< .01) and abuse as a whole (r = –.42, P< .01).

Table 3.21: Shows relationship between marital conflict, life stress, women empowerment and various forms of domestic violence.

Dimensions of Domestic Violence	*Physical Abuse*	*Sexual Abuse*	*Psychological Abuse*	*Economic Abuse*	*D.A. (Abuse) As a whole*
PMarital Conflict	.61**	.43**	.62**	.59**	.68**
Life Stress	.53**	.35**	.55**	.54**	.60**
Women Empowerment	-.32**	-.29**	-.42**	-.30**	-.42**

N = 140, **P < .01, *P < .05

Results, thus, indicate that with increasing empowerment level in women the level of domestic violence decreased.

Results, thus confirm the roles of socio-psychological variables in the origin and sustenance of violence against women behind closed doors.

Impact of Domestic Violence on Children

Consequences of the exposure to domestic violence were investigated under 4th and 5th objectives of the study. Obtained results are interpreted in this section.

Fourth objective of this study was to investigate the linkages between Domestic Violence and incidence of child abuse. Data obtained from children were treated statistically in terms of comparative, correlational and Stepwise Multiple Regression analyses respectively. Results are displayed in Table 3.22 and Figure 3.17 and reported below:

Table 3.22: Means, SDs and 't'–values for various forms of child abuse between exposed and unexposed groups of children.

Dimensions of Domestic Violence	*Exposed Mean*	*Unexposed Mean*	*t*
Physical Abuse	20.27	18.40	.654
Psychological Abuse	40.55	30.55	2.40*
Sexual Abuse	12.04	5.48	3.20**
Economic Abuse	17.23	11.00	2.74*
Physical Neglect	13.15	9.19	2.71*
Emotional Neglect	15.29	8.71	3.98**
Educational Neglect	18.10	11.86	2.75**
Abuse As a whole	136.35	95.02	3.22**

** P<.01, * P<.05

(A) Domestic Violence and Child Abuse

Results displayed in Table 3.22 and Fig. 3.17 denote significant differences on various forms of child abuse between exposed and unexposed groups of children. Significant 't' value on abuse as a whole [t (118) = 3.22, P< .000], suggests that exposed children were found highly abused than unexposed children. Similarly, significant 't'values for psychological abuse [t (118) = 3.40, P< .01], sexual abuse [t (118) = 3.20, P< .01], economic abuse [t (118) = 2.74, P< .01], physical neglect [t (118) = 2.71, P< .01], educational neglect [t (118) = 2.75, P< .01] and emotional neglect [t (118) = 3.98, P< .001] are also significant. Results evince that exposed group of children were found highly abused and neglected (M. Psy) = (40.55), Sex. = (12.04), Eco. = (17.23), Edu. = (18.10), Emo. = (15.29) than unexposed group of children [M Psy. = (30.55), Sex = (5.48), Edu. Neg. = (11.86.) and Emo. Negl. = (8.71)] respectively.

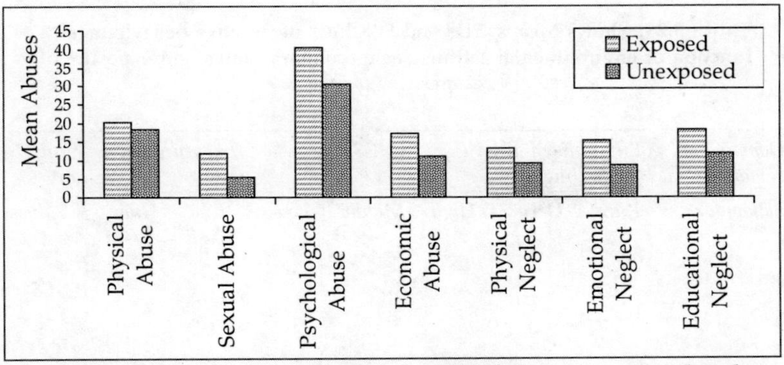

Fig. 3.17: Displays various forms of child abuse in exposed and unexposed groups of children

Findings, thus, suggest that the exposure of domestic violence also causes detrimental role in high incidence of child abuse and neglect.

(B) Domestic Violence and Child Behaviour

Fifth objective of the study was to investigate the impact of domestic violence on behavioural functioning of children.

Data obtained on Child Behaviour Questionnaire were scored according to defined rules and treated statistically in terms of comparative, correlational and Step-wise Multiple Regression Analyses. Results are displayed in Tables and Figures respectively.

In order to assess the influence of residential setting, socio-economic status and exposure level of domestic violence on a set of child behaviours a 2 × 3 × 2 factorial analysis of variance (Rural—Urban Setting X High, Middle-Low SES X

Exposed-Unexposed groups) was computed for each form of behaviour. Results obtained on each behaviour, are displayed in Tables and Figures and interpreted below:

(i) Aggression—Results (Table 3.23) indicate a significant main effect for exposure level [F(1,119) = 24.34, P< .01] which reveals that children exposed to domestic violence expressed heightened level of aggression (M = 561.67) than children not exposed to domestic violence (M = 479.23).

Table 3.23: Shows Means, SDs and F-'values' of negative behaviours as a function of environmental setting, socio-economic status and exposure of domestic violence

Domains of Negative	*Environmental Setting*		*SES*			*Exposure Level*		*Signifi-cant*
Behaviour	*Rural*	*Urban*	*High*	*Middle*	*Low*	*Ex-posed*	*Unex-posed*	*F Values A-setting B-SES C-Exposure*
Aggression								
M	**518.48**	**522.41**	**523.07**	**509.40**	**528.87**	**561.67**	**479.23**	**C=**
SD	**11.10**	**12.50**	**13.81**	**13.67**	**15.84**	**9.75**	**13.58**	**24.34****
Non Compliance								
M	**33.23**	**34.98**	**33.51**	**32.82**	**35.98**	**34.29**	**33.92**	**AXB=**
SD	**.82**	**.93**	**1.02**	**1.01**	**1.72**	**.72**	**1.00**	**3.46***
Destructive Behaviour								
M	**27.55**	**26.64**	**26.47**	**24.38**	**30.44**	**28.05**	**26.13**	**B=4.30***
SD	**1.10**	**1.24**	**1.37**	**1.36**	**1.57**	**.97**	**1.35**	**AXC= 4.50***
Bullying								
M	**29.45**	**29.39**	**29.0**	**27.31**	**31.35**	**31.98**	**26.86**	**C= 8.68****
SD	**1.15**	**1.30**	**1.44**	**1.42**	**1.65**	**1.01**	**1.41**	**AXB= 4.16* AXC= 10.48****

****P < .01, *P < .05**

(ii) Non-Compliance: Results displayed in Table 3.23 further shows that on non-compliance, setting x S.E.S. (A x B) interaction effect [F(2,119) = 3.46, P< .05] is found significant. The interaction graph (Fig. 3.18) evinces that in case of rural sample, non-compliance was found maximum in middle class than low and high SES respectively. However, the reverse pattern was found in case of urban sample. Maximum non-compliance was identified in low SES children than high and middle class counterparts respectively.

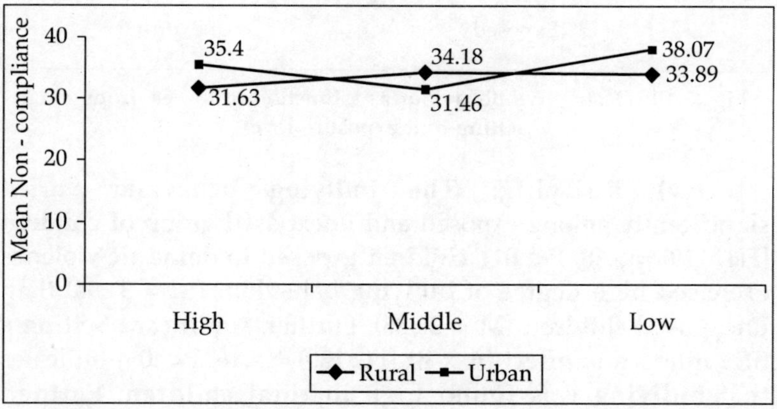

Fig. 3.18: Non-compliance as a function of interaction of environmental setting and socio-economic status

(iii) Destructive Behaviour—Results (Table 3.23) indicate a significant main effect for socio-economic status [F(2,119) = 4.30, P< .05] which reveals that low SES children showed more destructive behaviour (M = 30.44) than the high (M = 26.47) and middle SES children (M = 24.38). However, exposure of domestic violence x setting interaction effect [F(1, 119) = 4.50, P< .05] was found significant. The interaction graph (Fig. 3.19) shows that in case of rural children, destructive behaviour was found maximum in exposed group than unexposed children. However, the reverse pattern was found in case of urban sample.

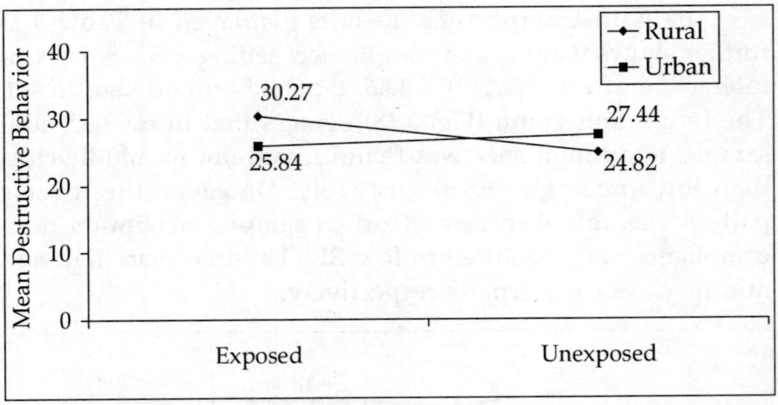

Fig. 3.19: Destructive Behaviour as a function of the environmental setting and exposure level

(iv) Bullying: The bullying behaviour varied significantly among exposed and unexposed group of children [F(1, 119) = 8.68, P< .01], children exposed to domestic violence exercised high degree of bullying behaviour (M = 31.98) than unexposed children (M = 26.86). Further, significant Setting x SES interaction effect (A x B) [F(2,120) = 4.16, P< .05] indicates that bullying was found high in rural children. Further, interaction graph (Fig. 3.20a) evinces that in case of urban sample, bullying behaviour was found maximum in low S.E.S. group than high and middle S.E.S. children respectively. However, the reverse pattern was found in case of rural

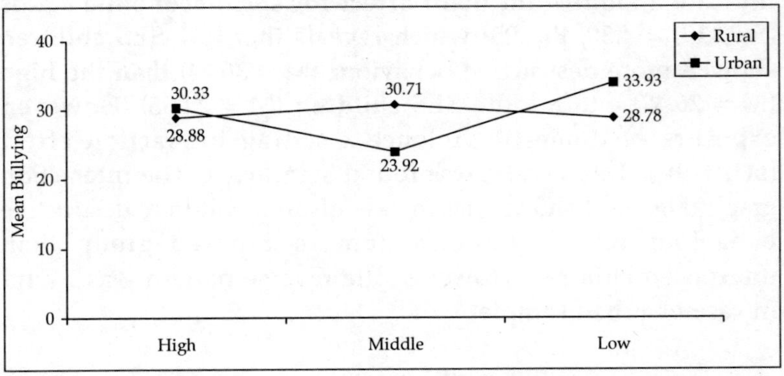

Fig. 3.20 (a): Bullying as a function of the environmental setting and socio-economic status

children, maximum bullying behaviour was displayed by middle class than low and high class children respectively. The residential setting x exposure level (A x C) interaction effect (Fig. 3.20b) was also found significant (F(1,119) = 10.48, P< .01) which denotes that in case of urban setting, little difference was found between unexposed and exposed children. However, in case of rural children, greater level of bullying in exposed children than unexposed children.

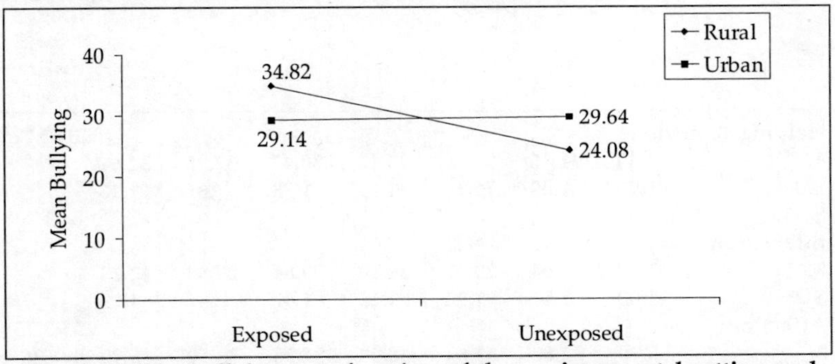

Fig. 3.20 (b): Bullying as a function of the environmental setting and exposure level

(v) Helping Behaviour—Table 3.24 shows the Means, SDs and F-values on helping behaviour. The significant main effect for SES [F(2,119) = 3.72, P< .05] indicates that middle class children showed maximum helping behaviour (M = 35.12) than high (M = 31.70) and low SES (M = 30.47) children respectively. However, residential setting and exposure level were found non-significant..

(vi) Social Interaction—On social interaction, significant F-value for SES [F(2,119) = 3.79, P< .05] reveals that middle class children showed higher level of social interaction (M = 33.80) than low (M = 29.84) and high SES children (M = 29.37) respectively. Residential setting and exposure of domestic violence did not exercise significant impact on social interaction.

(vii) Affection—ANOVA result (Table 3.24) evinced a significant main effect for setting [F(1,119) = 3.23, P< .05] which shows that rural children displayed more affection (M = 35.70) than their urban counterparts (M = 32.89). Further, significant

Table 3.24: Shows Means, SDs and F-'values' of positive behaviours as a function of exposure of D.V., environmental setting and socio-economic status

Domains of Positive	*Environmental Setting*		*Socio - economic Status*			*Exposure Level*		*Significant*
Behaviour	*Rural*	*Urban*	*High*	*Middle*	*Low*	*Exposed*	*Unexposed*	*F Value A-Setting B=SES C=Exposure*
Helping Behaviour								**B=3.72***
M	**33.30**	**31.56**	**31.70**	**35.12**	**30.47**	**32.25**	**32.61**	
SD	**.96**	**1.09**	**1.20**	**1.19**	**1.38**	**.85**	**1.18**	
Social Interaction								**B=3.79***
M	**31.07**	**30.94**	**29.37**	**33.80**	**29.84**	**29.88**	**32.13**	
SD	**1.00**	**1.12**	**1.24**	**1.23**	**1.42**	**.87**	**1.22**	
Affection								**A=3.23***
M	**35.70**	**32.89**	**33.64**	**38.00**	**31.25**	**33.50**	**35.10**	**B=6.36****
SD	**1.04**	**1.17**	**1.29**	**1.28**	**1.48**	**.91**	**1.27**	**AxBxC =2.99***
Discipline								**B=3.81**
M	**33.03**	**32.72**	**31.41**	**36.44**	**30.80**	**31.03**	**34.74**	**C=3.92***
SD	**1.24**	**1.40**	**1.55**	**1.53**	**1.78**	**1.09**	**1.52**	**AxC =5.52***
Reciprocal Relationship								**AxBxC =4.94****
M	**30.44**	**30.96**	**30.18**	**31.65**	**30.27**	**30.09**	**31.31**	
SD	**.73**	**.82**	**.91**	**.90**	**1.04**	**.64**	**.90**	
Task Involvement								**C=5.52* AxC**
M	**38.05**	**38.57**	**38.57**	**39.24**	**37.11**	**37.09**	**39.53**	**=5.06***
SD	**.69**	**.78**	**.86**	**.85**	**.99**	**.61**	**.85**	**AxBxC =6.39****
Study Behaviour								**B=4.87** C=5.43***
M	**27.34**	**26.74**	**27.38**	**23.09**	**30.65**	**24.75**	**29.32**	**AxB =2.83***
SD	**1.30**	**1.47**	**1.62**	**1.60**	**1.86**	**1.14**	**1.59**	**AxC= 11.58****

****P < .01, *P < .05**

main effect for SES [F(2,119) = 6.36, P< .01] which reveals that low SES children expressed poor affection level, (M = 31.25) than high (M = 33.64) and middle SES children (M = 38.00) respectively. However, setting and exposure influence were non-significant. Despite this, AxBxC interaction effect [F(2,119) = 2.99, P< .05], (Fig.3.21) reveals that in case of exposed children, affection behaviour was very low in rural and urban children of low SES than high and middle SES children respectively. While in case of unexposed group rural and urban children of middle SES showed higher affection level than high and low SES children.

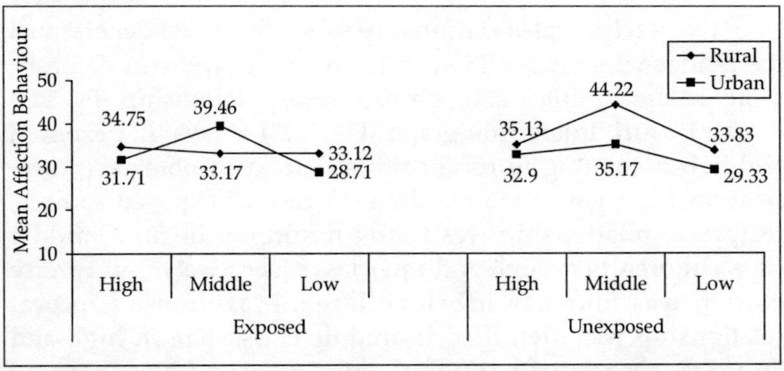

Fig. 3.21: Affection behaviour as a function of three way interaction of environmental setting, socio-economic status and exposure level.

(viii) Discipline—As Table (3.24) indicates that on discipline domain, significant main effect for SES [F(2,119) = 3.81, P< .05] reveals that discipline was found very poor in low SES children (M = 30.80) than high (M = 31.41) and middle SES children (M = 36.44) respectively. The impact of the exposure of domestic violence was also found significant [F(1,119) = 3.92, P< .05]. ANOVA result evinces that children exposed to domestic violence were found low disciplined (M= 31.03) than unexposed (M = 34.74) children. Significant environmental setting x exposure interaction effect [F(1,119) = 5.52, P< .05] (Fig.3.22) indicates that discipline was found poor in exposed children belonging to rural setting however, in case of unexposed children, the reverse pattern was found in urban children.

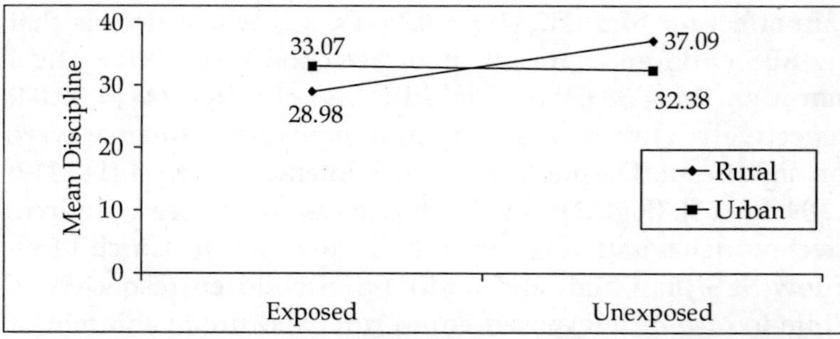

Fig. 3.22: Discipline as a function of the environmental setting and exposure level.

(ix) Reciprocal-Relationship –As Table (3.24) denotes that the residential setting, SES of children and exposure of domestic violence have joint impact on reciprocal relationship [F(2,119) = 4.94, P< .01]. Interaction graph (Fig. 3.23) shows that exposed children belonging to rural setting displayed poor reciprocal relationship than urban children. In case of exposed sample, reciprocal relationship was found minimum in rural middle class children than high and low class respectively, but reverse pattern was found in urban children. Maximum reciprocal relationship was identified in middle class, than in high and low class respectively. Despite this, in case of Non-exposed group, reciprocal relationship was minimum in low SES than in middle and high SES urban children but in case of rural setting, maximum level of reciprocal relationship was found in middle class than in high and low class children respectively.

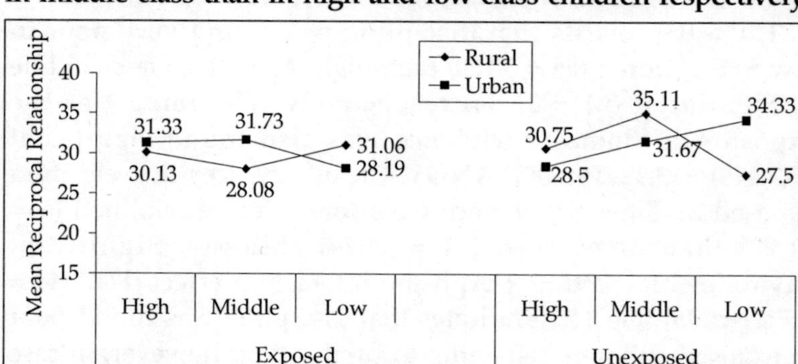

Fig. 3.23: Reciprocal Relationship as a function of three way interaction of environmental setting, socio-economic status and exposure level.

(x) Task Involvement—The responses on task involvement also differed significantly across exposed and unexposed groups (Table 3.24). The significant main effect for exposure level [F(1,119) = 5.52, P< .05] evinced that exposed children showed poor task involvement (M = 37.09) than unexposed children (M = 39.53). Significant residential setting x exposure of domestic violence interaction effect [F(1,119) = 5.06, P< .05] (Fig. 3.24a) denotes that exposed children of both settings (rural and urban) expressed low task involvement than unexposed children. Significant residential setting × SES × exposure level interaction effect [F(2,119)= 6.39, P< .01] and interaction graph (Fig. 3.24b) reveal that in case of exposed children, task involvement was very low in rural and low SES than high and middle SES children respectively, but in case of urban setting, middle class children showed more task involvement than high and low SES children respectively. While, in case of unexposed group rural children of middle SES showed high task involvement than high and low SES children but in urban setting, low SES children showed more task involvement than high and middle SES children respectively.

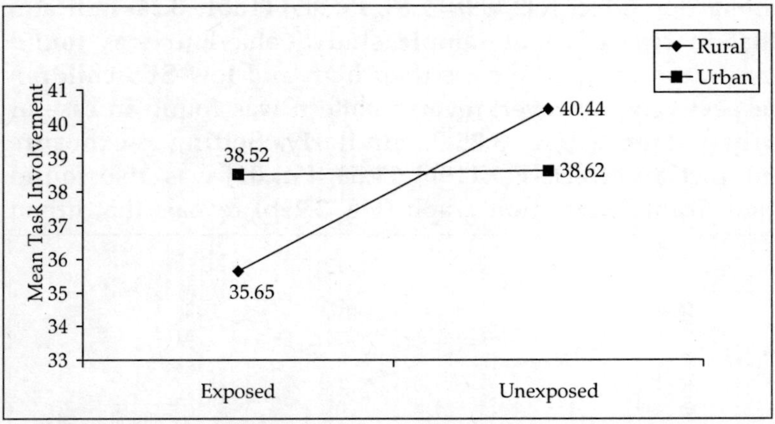

Fig. 3.24(a): Task Involvement as a function of the environmental setting and exposure level.

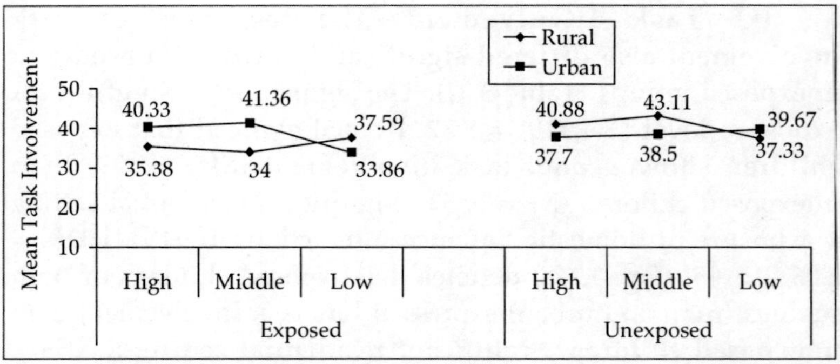

Fig. 3.24(b): Task Involvement as a function of three way interaction of level of environmental setting, socio-economic status and exposure level.

(xi) Study Behaviour—Results displayed in Table 3.24 evinces that main effect for SES was found significant on study behaviour [F(2,119)= 4.87, P< .01]. The result indicates that the study behaviour was found significantly higher in low SES (M= 30.65) than high (M= 27.38) and middle (M= 23.09) SES respectively. Likewise, the significant exposure level [F(1,118) = 5.43, P< .05] evinced that exposed children showed diminished study behaviour (M = 24.74) than unexposed children (M = 29.32). Further, significant Setting × SES interaction effect [F(2,119)= 2.83, P< .05] (Table 3.24) indicates that in case of rural sample study behaviour was found maximum in middle class than high and low SES children respectively, however, reverse pattern was found in case of urban sample (Fig. 3.25a). Similarly, Setting x exposure interaction effect [F(1,119)= 11.58, P< .01] was also found significant. Interaction graph (Fig. 3.25b) reveals that urban

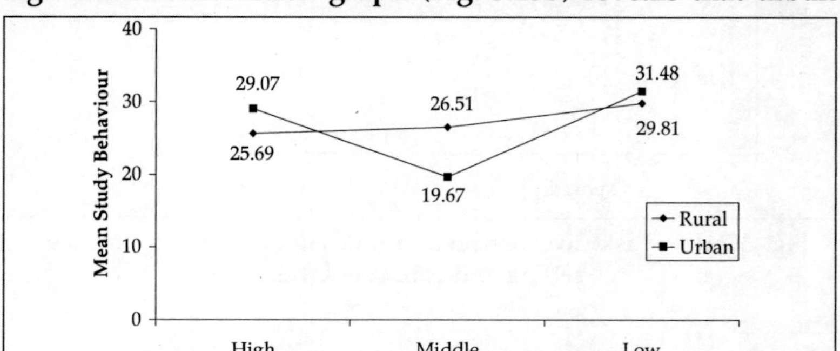

Fig. 3.25(a): Study Behaviour as a function of the environmental setting and socio-economic status.

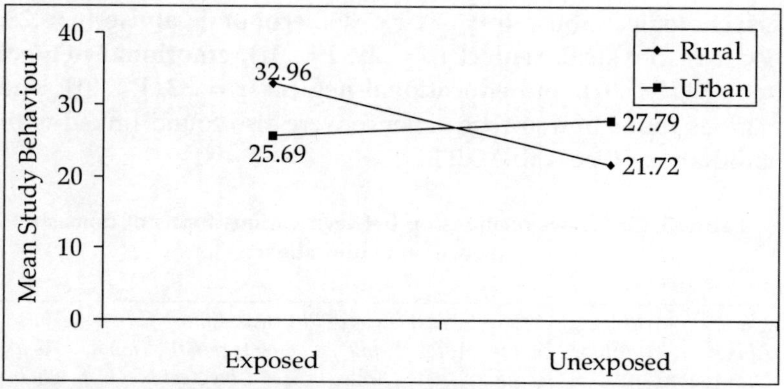

Fig. 3.25(b): Study Behaviour as a function of the environmental setting and exposure level.

children, exposed to domestic violence were found inferior in study behaviour than unexposed children however, in case of rural sample reverse pattern was found.

Correlation Analysis

In order to obtain further insight into the linkages among variables, correlational analysis was done for child sample. Correlations were computed to ascertain:

(I) The relationship between domestic violence and child abuse viz., physical abuse, psychological abuse, sexual abuse, economic abuse, physical neglect, educational neglect, emotional neglect and abuse as a whole.

(II) The relationship of domestic violence with various forms of behavioural functioning viz., helping behaviour, social-interaction, aggression, non-compliance, destructive behaviour, affection, discipline, reciprocal relationship, task involvement, bullying and study behaviour.

(I) Relationship between Domestic Violence and Child Abuse—Correlations were computed between various forms of domestic violence and child abuse. Results displayed in Table 3.25 denotes exclusively positive relationship between domestic violence and various forms of child abuse. The exposure of domestic violence was found to be positively correlated with child abuse as a whole ($r = .30$, $P < .01$), psychological abuse (r = .20, P< .05), economic abuse (r = .28, P< .01), physical neglect (r = .29, P< .01), emotional neglect (r = .31, P< .01), and educational neglect (r = .33, P< .01). The various forms of domestic violence were also found linked with child abuse (See Table 3.25).

Table 3.25: Shows relationship between various forms of domestic violence and child abuse.

Child Abuse Dimensions of Domestic Violence	*Physical Abuse*	*Psy-chological Abuse*	*Sexual Abuse*	*Econo-mic Abuse*	*Physical Neglect*	*Emo-tional Neglect*	*Educa-tional Neglect*	*Abuse As a whole*
Physical Abuse	.08	.24**	.11	.27**	.26**	.28**	.29**	.29**
Sexual Abuse	.05	.09	.15	.17	.22*	.17	.14	.18*
Psycholo-gical Abuse	.12	.23*	.12	.26**	.31**	.31**	.28**	.30**
Economic Abuse	-.02	.17	.16	.19*	.28**	.20*	.27**	.23*
D.A. (abuse) as a whole	.04	.20*	.15	.28**	.29**	.31**	.33**	.30**

N = 120, **P< .01, *P< .05

(II) Relationship between Domestic Violence and Child Behaviour— Results displayed in Table 3.26, evince that exposure level of D.V. was found negatively correlated with positive behaviours. More specifically, helping behaviour was found negatively correlated with physical abuse (r = –.32, P< .01), sexual abuse (r = –.26, P< .01), psychological abuse (r = –.21,P< .05), economic abuse (r = –.30, P< .01) and abuse as a whole (r = –.25, P< .01). Similarly, social interaction was found negatively correlated with physical abuse (r = –.21, P< .05), sexual abuse (r = –.18, P< .05), psychological abuse (r = –.18, P< .05) and abuse as a whole (r = –.19, P< .05) respectively. Affection behaviour was also found negatively correlated with physical abuse (r = –.18, P< .05), sexual abuse (r = –.20, P< .05), economic abuse(r = –.21, P< .05). Further, task involvement was found inversely related with psychological abuse (r = –.19, P< .05) and abuse as a whole (r = –.18, P< .05). Discipline was also found negatively correlated (r = –.20, P< .05) with exposure of domestic violence. Despite this, positive but low relationship between negative behaviours and exposure of violence was identified (Table 3.26).

Table 3.26: Shows relationship between various forms of domestic violence and child behaviour.

Domestic Violence Child Behaviours	*Physical Abuse*	*Sexual Abuse*	*Psycho-logical Abuse*	*Economic Abuse*	*Abuse as a whole*
Aggression	.16	.15	.08	.11	.11
Non compliance	.17	.04	.12	.11	.09
Destructive Behaviour	.14	.09	.14	.11	.09
Bullying	.07	.05	.05	.08	.05
Helping Behaviour	-.32**	-.26**	-.21*	-.30**	–.25**
Social Interaction	-.21*	-.18*	-.18*	-.10	-.19*
Affection	-.18*	-.20*	-.14	-.21*	-.13
Discipline	-.15	-.16	-.09	-.20*	-.07
Reciprocal Relationship	-.07	-.05	-.06	-.12	-.07
Task Involvement	-.17	-.17	-.19*	-.15	-.18*
Study Behaviour	.04	.08	.06	.05	.002

N = 120, **P< .01, *P< .05

Step-Wise Multiple Regression Analysis (SMRA)

Based on perusal of correlation results, it was considered appropriate to go for Step-Wise Multiple Regression Analysis (SWRA) to examine the relative contributions of antecedent factors to criterion variables. Findings of these analyses are in the following order:

(i) Predictions of Child Abuse by Domestic Violence

Since, correlations between domestic violence and child abuse were found significant, thus, it was considered adequate to

calculate Step-wise Multiple Regression Analysis (SWRA) to examine the relative contributions of various forms of domestic violence to child abuse. The findings of this analysis are in order.

As regression result (Table 3.27) indicates that child abuse (as a whole) was significantly explained by domestic violence (DV). Women's psychological abuse contributed maximum positively (β = .30, R^2 = .09). In other words domestic violence (Psy) explained 9% variance in the criterion variable

Table 3.27: Stepwise Multiple Regression Analysis for Abuse as a whole as predicted by domestic violence (psychological)

Predictors	*Criterion*					
	R	*R^2*	*R^2 Change*	*Beta (β)*	*t*	*F*
			Child abuse (as a whole)			
Domestic Violence (Psychological)	**.30**	**.09**	**.09**	**.30**	**3.45**	**11.85****
			Child Psychological Abuse			
Domestic Violence (Physical)	**.25**	**.06**	**.06**	**.25**	**2.73**	**7.46****
Domestic Violence (as a whole)	**.28**	**.14**	**.08**	**.28**	**3.22**	**10.35****
			Child Physical Neglect			
Domestic Violence (Psychological)	**.31**	**.10**	**.10**	**.31**	**3.52**	**12.39****
			Child Emotional Neglect			
Domestic Violence (Psychological)	**.31**	**.10**	**.10**	**.31**	**3.54**	**12.51****
Domestic Violence (as a whole)	**.33**	**.11**	**.11**	**.33**	**3.79**	**14.33****

****P<.01, *P<.05**

(child abuse), whereas child psychological abuse was predicted by domestic violence (physical) (β = .25, R^2 = .06), followed by domestic violence as a whole (β = .28, R^2 = .14). Thus, domestic

violence (physical abuse) explained 6%, while domestic violence (as a whole) explained 8 % of variance, but composite contributions of these factors were found 14% variance in the criterion variable (child psychological abuse). It appears that high exposure of domestic violence (physical abuse of mother) predicted high incidences of child psychological abuses. It is apparent from table that child physical neglect was significantly predicted by domestic violence (women's psychological abuse). Women's psychological abuse contributed maximum positively (β = .31, R^2 = .10). Results, thus suggest that exposure of domestic violence (women's psychological abuse) contributed 10% of variance in high incidence of child physical neglect. Results (table 3.27) further evinced that child emotional neglect was predicted by domestic violence (psychological abuse) which contributed maximum positively (β = .31, R^2 = .10). In other words, women's psychological abuse explained 10% of variance in the emotional neglect of children. Regression results (Table 3.27) again revealed that child educational neglect was predicted by domestic violence (abuse as a whole) maximum positively (β = .33, R^2 = .11). In other words, domestic violence explained 11% of variance in the criterion variable. Results thus, suggest that exposure of various forms of domestic violence contributed high incidences of child abuse and neglect.

(ii) Prediction of Child Behaviour by Child Abuse and Domestic Violence

On the basis of correlation results, it was viewed essential to calculate Step Wise Multiple Regression Analysis (SWMR) to examine the relative contributions of child abuse and domestic violence to child behaviour.

Table 3.28 : Step Wise Multiple Regression Analysis of Child Behaviour on to the various forms of Domestic Violence and Child Abuse.

Predictors	*Criterion*					
	R	R^2	R^2 *Change*	*Beta* (ß)	*t*	*F*
			Helping Behaviour			
Domestic violence	.42	.13	.05	-.23	2.64	12.72**
Child Abuse (as a whole)	.36	.18	.13	-.36	4.20	17.62**
Child Emotional Neglect	.47	.22	.04	-.32	2.44	10.83**
			Social Interaction			
Domestic violence (as a whole)	.21	.05	.05	-.21	2.35	5.53**
			Reciprocal Relationship			
Child Abuse (as a whole)	.35	.12	.12	-.35	4.06	16.47**
			Affection			
Child Abuse (as a whole)	.43	.18	.18	-.43	5.17	26.76**
			Discipline			
Child Abuse (as a whole)	.41	.17	.17	-.41	4.91	24.12**
			Task Involvement			
Domestic violence	.45	.20	.03	-.21	1.99	14.63**
Child Abuse (as a whole)	.44	.17	.17	-.42	4.97	24.69**
			Study Behaviour			
Child Emotional Neglect	.37	.13	.13	-.37	4.27	18.23**
			Non Compliance			
Child Psychological Neglect	.28	.08	.08	.28	3.12	9.76**
			Bullying			
Child Abuse (as a whole)	.34	.11	.11	.34	3.86	14.94**
			Aggression			
Child Abuse (as a whole)	.32	.10	.10	.32	3.68	13.51**
			Destructive Behaviour			
Child Abuse (as a whole)	.43	.18	.18	.43	5.12	26.20**

****P<.01, *P<.05**

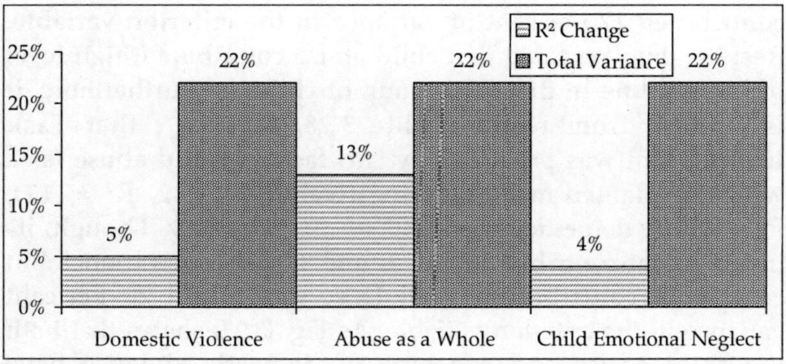

Fig. 3.26: Prediction of Helping Behaviour by Child Abuse and Domestic Violence

As is apparent from the result (Table 3.28 & Figure 3.26), 'Helping Behaviour' was predicted by three factors. Child abuse as a whole predicted maximum negatively (β = –.36, R^2 = .13) followed by domestic violence (Women's physical abuse) (β = .23, R^2 = .18). Contrary to this, child helping behaviour was explained positively by child's emotional neglect (β = .32, R^2 =.22). Independent contributions of these factors are in order : Child abuse as a whole explained 13 per cent, while domestic violence (physical abuse) explained 5 per cent and child emotional neglect explained only 4 per cent of variance but composite contributions of these factors were found 22 per cent variance in the criterion variable. Regression result, further denotes that child's 'Social Interaction' was negatively explained by domestic violence (physical abuse) (β = .21, R^2 = .05) which contributed 5 per cent variance in the criterion variable. Regression result, further indicates that 'Reciprocal Relationship' was predicted negatively by child physical neglect (β= -.35, R^2 = .12), which contributed 12 per cent of variance in the criterion variable. Results show that child abuse contributed poor reciprocal relationship in children.

Similarly, child 'Affection Behaviour' was also negatively predicted by child abuse (β = .43, R^2 = .18), which contributed 18 per cent variance in the criterion variable which was the only significant predictor of affection. Likewise, Discipline was negatively predicted by child abuse (β = -.41, R^2 = .17), which

contributed 17 per cent of variance in the criterion variable. Results, thus, revealed that child abuse contributed high level of indiscipline in different group of children. Furthermore, it is evident from result (Table 3.28, Fig. 3.27) that Task Involvement was predicted by two factors. Child abuse (as a whole) explained maximum negatively (β = -.42, R^2 = .17), followed by domestic violence (β = -.21, R^2 = .03). Though, its independent contribution was found 17 per cent variance but composite contribution with D.V. was found 20 per cent variance in the criterion variable. As Fig. (3.27) shows that both the child abuse and exposure of domestic violence have contributed inversely in the task involvement of children. Regression result further indicates that 'Study Behaviour' was negatively predicted by child's emotional neglect (β = -.37, R^2 = .13), which contributed 13 per cent variance in the criterion variable which was the only significant predictor of study behaviour.

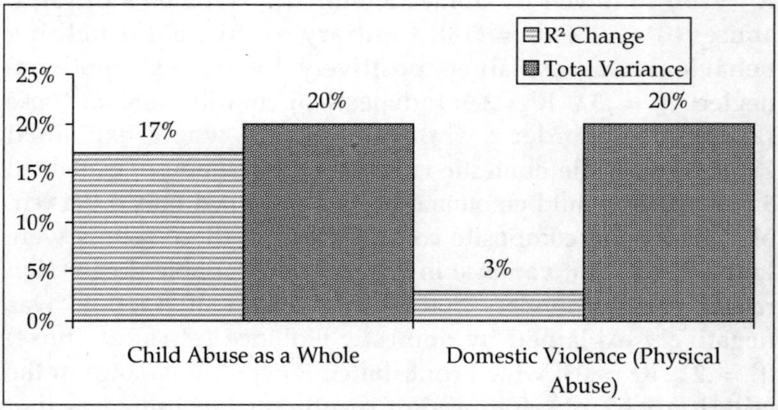

Fig. 3.27: Prediction of task involvement by child abuse and domestic violence.

Contrary to this, 'Non-Compliance' was positively predicted by child psychological abuse (β .28, R^2 = .08) which contributed 8 per cent variance in the criterion variable. Bullying was also positively predicted by child abuse (β = .34, R^2 = .11), which contributed 11 per cent variance in the criterion variable. Present result further evinced that Aggression was predicted by child abuse positively (β = .32, R^2 = .10), which

contributed 10 per cent of variance in the criterion variable. Results, thus, indicate that child abuse predicted high aggression level in children. Similarly, Destructive Behaviour was significantly predicted by child abuse as a whole (β = .43, R^2 = .18), which contributed 18 per cent of variance in the criterion variable. Findings, thus, suggest that high incidence of child abuse contributes more destructive behaviour in children. Results thus, indicate that domestic violence and child abuse contribute negative role in the development of behavioural problems in children.

Present findings reveal that certain social and psychological factors play significant role in the origin and sustenance of domestic violence and the exposure of domestic violence to children cause high incidence of child abuse and behavioural problems in children.

Furthermore, to understand the forms, causative factors and magnitude of domestic violence in different strata of society, case study was done. Case Histories of respondents are reported in second section of the chapter.

SECTION II: RESULTS

Case Histories

This section presents twelve case histories of domestic violence victims from rural and urban areas of Gorakhpur. Although, they are heavily disguised to retain anonymity, but the abuses by husband/family members (viz. physical, sexual, psychological and economic) are exactly as described. In each case, the essential features of domestic violence which is prominent in the definition, namely, its sustained repetitive nature, has been emphasized. Some indication of the length of time, the abuse has been developing, and of its origins, would be provided, as numerous observations of its existing impact upon the women's physical and social development along with its consequences on children. Together with the empirical observations and foundations already laid in earlier part of the chapter, these case histories would be helpful in understanding the causative roots of domestic violence and constructing a conceptual framework for easy references in identifying incidences and causative roots of domestic violence in Gorakhpur region or eastern districts of Uttar Pradesh in particular and at national level in general.

Case I (Vimala)

This narrative is reported by a 40 yrs. old urban female (house wife) of middle S.E.S., married at the early age of 16, lives with her husband and children in Gorakhpur city. Her husband is working in police department. She has three children (1 daughter and 2 sons). Her husband is an acute alcoholic. After heavy drinking, he throws things out of the house also hits, kicks and beats his wife and children and tortures them physically, sexually and psychologically. His daughter is often sexually abused by her father. He exposes his internal organs to his daughter, embraces her and touches her body forcefully, and tries to make sexual relationship with her. Whenever, his wife checks him to not to do such acts with own daughter, he assaults her physically and psychologically.

He has broken T.V. by throwing it and has stopped providing household necessities. Thus, they are living in high scarcity. He spends all his earning in drinking and fulfilling his desires. Often he behaves destructively viz.; torn his clothes, throws water on bed and beats everyone without any reason. He beats his son 'Anurag' excessively. He also abuses and neglects children and does not pay attention on their education. He usually throws all the cooking material outside of house and says its better if she (wife) dies that he could remarry any other women.

Abuses of Vimala:

Physical Abuses:	Hitting, kicking, beating and throwing out by husband.
Sexual Abuses:	Trying to make sexual relations with own daughter, forcefully catches or touches sex organs of her daughter, exposes own sex organs to her
Psychological Abuses:	Name calling, embarrassment, threatening of death, terrorizing her and children.
Economic Abuses:	No financial support to wife and family for household necessities, financial scarcity and misuse of money by husband.
Consequences:	Highly stressed, shows symptoms of depression, frustration and distress, daughter is depressed, her familial and social life seriously affected, self-destructive behaviour, guilt feeling, feeling of helplessness, fear of social alienation etc.

Case II (Meera Pandey)

Meera Pandey, a 25 year old Brahmin lady, was married at an early age of 15. She lives with her husband in Gorakhpur city, who is a driver. She has three children; one son and two daughters. This lady is severely abused by her husband and in-laws. Earlier, she lived with her in-laws, they started torturing her mentally in many ways (quarrelling, sarcastic comments, name calling etc.). They planned to separate her from the family. Even she was not given food for three days and her children were also unfed during those days. Her in-laws continuously abused her. On 30th June, 2006, they tried to kill her, by pushing her down the roof. They sold her share of property (land etc.). For them, her husband also abuses her physically and psychologically. Her husband and in-laws beat her for small things and always quarrel with her. In fact, her husband is a heavy drunkard. Once her husband and in-laws tried to burn her by putting kerosene oil on her body, but with the intervention of neighbours, she was saved and escaped to her maternal family. The lady was praying for the direct intervention of Police. The lady was ignorant of legal protection against domestic violence.

Abuses of Meera Pandey

Physical Abuses:	Physical assault, attempted to push down the roof, tried to burn her by putting kerosene oil on her body by husband and in-laws.
Psychological Abuses:	Threatening to death, non-cooperation, no emotional support, name calling, mental torture.
Economic Abuses:	Thrown out of paternal house, her in-laws sold her share of property.
Consequences:	Highly depressed, high feeling of stress and insecurity, poor physical health and no social interaction.

Case III (Renu Agrawal)

Renu Agrawal is a housewife of 28 years age. She is a graduate and belongs to high socio-economic status. Her husband is a businessman and owns a shop of motor parts. She has two children (one son and one daughter). She is victimized by her in-laws. Narratives of Renu are reported below:

Narratives: "After a few days of marriage, my mother-in-law started abusing me for household work. The abuse increased day by day. When my husband comes from the shop, she provokes him by telling false stories about me and makes him furious, then my husband starts beating me after drinking heavily. My father-in-law wants me to exploit sexually. Once, I was alone in my house (as my mother-in-law had gone to her maternal home and my husband and brother-in-law had gone to shop) my father-in-law drunken, entered my room and tried to catch and sexually assault me. He pushed me on the bed and uncovered me. I screamed and prayed him to leave me but everything was unheard. Fortunately, I got the lamp and threw it on him and ran away to another room and locked it. Then I called my husband and my brother. When my husband came my father-in-law blamed me by calling me prostitute. My brother came at that moment and I went to my maternal home."

"After two weeks (10-15 days) my mother-in-law came back, I met and told her entire story. She supported me. My father-in-law came to me and apologized for his wrong doings. For several days, they tried to convince me to come back. Ultimately after 6 months, I came back to this house. Now, everything is going normal, only my husband and mother-in-law shout at me sometimes, whenever they get angry."

Abuses of Renu

Physical Abuses: Beating, pushing back, slapping by husband.

Sexual Abuses: Exploited by father-in-law, exposure of organs and unwanted touch by him and excessive sexual demand by husband.

Psychological Abuses: Name calling, threatening, embarrassment, no emotional support, self destruction.

Consequences: Feeling of insecurity, helplessness, social life seriously affected, high feeling of stress.

Case IV (Kundan Rai)

Kundan Rai, a 34 years old housewife, lives with her family in Gorakhpur city. She is highly educated, but is assaulted and severely abused by husband and in-laws. Now she wants divorce from her husband and some compensation for survival. She has five children; three daughters and two sons. Her husband is in police department. She is more educated than her husband and wants to do some job but her husband does not permit her. Since her husband regularly drinks liquor, therefore, his earning is insufficient for the fulfilment of family needs. He gives only, Rs. 1000.00 per month for household necessities which is not enough even for the school fees of the children. Her husband does not want to educate them more and when she sends children to school, he threats her to commit suicide. He does not beat her because he knows that if he will beat her, she will also beat him in return. Her husband spends all his money in drinking and when he has no money he sells food grains and cooking materials for buying liquor. Once, she complained to his senior officers and requested for intervention. She had gone to the DIG but could not get justice. He scolds her, uses dirty language which children do not understand. He wants to send her and his children to the village for the sake of free living. After falling drunken, he demands excessive sexual relationship and scolds her for that if she refuses, his ugly comments disturb her mental health.

Abuses of Kundan

Psychological Abuses: Husband suffers from inferiority complex and comments her sarcastically for high education, uses ugly language, no autonomy to excel

	in career and suppression of her abilities.
Sexual Abuses:	Exposure of organs, excessive demand for sex, unwanted touching.
Economic Abuses:	Severe financial scarcity, inadequate money for household, no money for school fees, high scarcity of basic necessities due to regular habit of liquor.
Consequences:	Depression, highly stressed, feeling of insecurity, no emotional support, embarrassment, de empowerment.

Case V [Sapana (name changed)]

This lady is 23 years old, at present living in a slum area of Gorakhpur city. She has married at an early age of 19 yrs. She is highly abused by her husband and cheated by him. Here is the story of her sufferings in her own narratives;

Narratives, "My parents fixed my marriage and my brother's marriage in a same house of Maharajganj" distt. (exchange marriage custom). My would be sister-in-law (bhabhi) was a divorce and mother of two children, thats' why my brother was not happy with this marriage. Before a few days of his marriage, he ran away with his faience to another city. To take revenge with my family, my in-laws earlier told nothing and accepted me as daughter-in-law a new member of the family. But it was a drama. After a few days, they started abusing me by scolding, name calling, hitting etc. My husband took me Delhi with him. At that time I was pregnant for 4 months. He said that he doesn't want the baby and it should be aborted but I refused. For this reason, he started to beat me. Forcefully, he gave me medicines to eat and after sometime, I lost my unborn child due to miscarriage. He was very happy and after a few days he left me for another woman. He took me back to Gorakhpur, left me and went back to Delhi. He has given only Rs. 100 to the landlord. For 8 months I waited for him, when I called him

(telephonically), he replied that if you are courageous then search me. I have not found him yet. Presently, he is living with that lady, who lives with her husband and two children. My husband sleeps with her (has sexual relation) but her husband says nothing just for money. I am living here hand-to-mouth and fulfilling my living by selling gold ornaments. My maternal family is not rich that's why they have not accepted me.

My earlier landlord demanded rent of the house, threatened me and also called me prostitute and threw my luggage with me out of the house. My neighbours helped me and took me to "Ranjana Saxena", the lawyer. She helped me to bring my things back from the landlord. Now, I am living in a new area where my neighbours help me a lot. They give me food to eat and clothes to wear. However, some people want to harass me.

Now, I want divorce from my husband but they (my in-laws) are not returning the money and things of my dowry. I am in conflict and want to do some job, to live independently and also trying for it.

Physical Abuses:	**Excessive beating, hitting, miscarriage, physical torture by throwing, kicking etc..**
Psychological Abuses:	**Scolding, name calling, no emotional support, extra marital affair and threatenings.**
Economic Abuses:	**No financial support from husband or in-laws, bound to live in hand-to-mouth, fulfills her necessities by selling ornaments.**
Consequences:	**Highly stressed, conflict and insecurity feeling, wants divorce, live in pathetic condition.**

Case VI (Vidyawati Devi)

Vidyawati Devi, a middle age (40 yrs.) housewife, lives with her family in the rural area of Gorakhpur city. She has four children (3 sons and 1 daughter). Her husband is unemployed and spends all his time in playing cards (gambling) and drinking liquor. If she interrupts and suggests to work, she gets hitting, kicking and dirty languages in response. Her husband is 5 yrs younger in age, that's why all the conflict and domestic violence is taking place. Each member of the family underestimates her. Her husband quarrels with her for liquor and this is the root cause of violence in this family. He spends all the money for buying liquor. Being unemployed, he is frustrated and abuses his wife. Everyone abuses her. Her husband does not take interest in children's education. A few months ago, she sold her gold ornaments to pay their fees, however her husband snatched half of her money and brought liquor. She is highly abused by in-laws and her husband and finds herself helpless.

Abuses of Vidyawati Devi

Physical Abuses:	**Hitting, kicking, excessive beating.**
Psychological Abuses:	**Name calling, quarrelling, dirty languages by husband and in-laws.**
Economic Abuses:	**No monetary support from husband even her husband snatches money, she sells her ornaments for children's school fees and bare necessities.**
Consequences:	**Frustration, depression, high conflict with husband, highly stressed, feeling of insecurity.**

Case VII (Sundari Yadav)

Sundari Yadav, a 30 yrs. old lady lives in the rural area of Gorakhpur city with her family. She has four children. After the birth of her last child, she completed her graduation and

this is the main cause of domestic violence. Her husband is educated up to 10th standard and due to jealousy, he insults her. She earns money by giving tuitions and stitching clothes. Her husband is a painter. During the sexual relationship only her husband poses to get listen her and understands her problems but after that he forgets everything. Her mother-in-law is the main cause of violence. She motivates her son to be dominating. She scolds her daughter-in-laws all the time. Any better or worse doing she says, her son follows it.

Abuses of Sundari Yadav

Physical Abuses:	Beating, kicking, throwing things, physical assault by mother-in-law and husband and therefore, miscarriage happened.
Psychological Abuses:	Name calling, emotional neglect. All forms of abuses committed by husband and mother in-law.
Consequences:	Highly stressed, high depression, frustration, de empowered.

Case VIII (Manju Dubey)

Manju Dubey, a 33 yrs. old housewife lives with her family in a rural area of Gorakhpur city. Her education is up to high school. She has two children and her husband works at a shop. Her mother-in-law and sister-in-law always scold her for not bringing enough dowry. Her husband also does not understand her feelings and always abuses her. Sometimes she thinks to commit suicide by taking poison. She was the only child of her parents and had brought lots of dowry with her. Here, in this house no body gives value to her. Her husband has beaten her once on the complaint of mother-in-law and sister-in-law, she fainted. Her daughter was very young at that time. Often her husband beats her for the household work. When her husband gets angry he kicks her out of the house and closes the door. When her neighbours interven then only he brings her back to home. Her father-in-law also abuses her.

Abuses of Manju

Physical Abuses:	Excessive beating, thrown out of house, kicking, slapping.
Psychological Abuses:	Mental torture, emotional abuse, no affection, regular harassments.
Economic Abuses:	High demand of dowry, further demand of money from parent's house.
Consequences:	Frustration, high depression and once, tried to commit suicide, insecurity and feeling of helplessness, poor physical and mental health status.

Case IX (Champa Devi)

Smt. Champa Devi a 32 yrs. old village woman, married at an early age of 10 yrs. is a severe victim of domestic violence. Her husband is an addict of liquor and after taking drinks, he abuses her frequently. She has six children (4 daughters and 2 sons). Her husband is unemployed and due to frustration he beats her excessively. Her husband passes whole time with the villagers by playing cards and drinking liquor. In the afternoon, when her husband comes back and if she asks anything, he starts scolding, beating and hitting her in front of family members.

Her husband does not trust her, if he finds her talking with any male person, he starts blaming by name calling or saying prostitute and scolds her excessively. Due to this action, she feels highly embarrassed infront of her children and neighbours.

Abuses of Champa

Physical Abuses:	**Kicking, hitting, slapping, excessive beating by husband.**
Psychological Abuses:	**Name calling (prostitute), no emotional support, emotional neglect, victims of husband's inferiority complex and frustrations.**
Economic Abuses:	**No monetary support from husband, he snatches her money, she sold her share of farm (landed property given by parents) to construct house.**
Consequences:	**Frustration, highly embarrassed, depression, no emotional support, highly stressed, social life severely affected.**

Case X (Reeta Yadav)

Reeta Yadav, a housewife of low strata, lives in a village with her family, she is the victim of domestic violence by husband and in-laws. She is highly abused by her husband. She was married at an early age of 7 yrs., now she is 28 yrs. old and her husband is 40. Her husband is an alcoholic and whenever she checks him for his wrong habits, he starts beating her. He has broken T.V. and other materials to terrorize her. Earlier, her husband was an employee in railway but now has been expelled from job and has no employment. He has spent all earnings in buying liquor. Reeta has three children (one daughter and two sons) but they are highly ignored by father. He does not take interest in their education, even does not want to educate them and he always abuses them. He beats his wife daily for no reason and whenever their children try to stop him, they are also physically assaulted by the father.

Abuses of Reeta Yadav

Physical Abuses:	Kicking, hitting, frequently slapping, and excessive beating, black spots and scar on the body of wife, child physical abuse by father.
Psychological Abuses:	Scolding, name calling, abusing all the time, no emotional support from husband and in-laws, educational neglect to children.
Economic Abuses:	No financial support from husband, very pathetic situation, bound to live in hand to mouth.
Consequences:	Highly stressed, embarrassment, feeling of insecurity, conflict with husband and family members, poor economic condition and bound to live in hand to mouth. Incidence of child abuse and neglect.

Case XI (Meera Gaur)

Meera Gaur, is a 45 yrs. old woman, working as maid servant. She belongs to low strata of society and resides with her family in slum area of Gorakhpur city. She was married at an early age of 13 yrs. and now has four children, two sons and two daughters. She is the high victim of domestic violence. Her mother-in-law and husband behave very badly with her. She is scolded and beaten by her husband very frequently. Whenever food is less or bad in taste, her husband and mother-in-law use to scold and start name calling (dirty comments). Her daughters help her in domestic work. She has taken loan on interest but now is unable to return it and for that she is in high stress all the time. Whatever she earns her husband takes forcefully and spends all the money in drinking liquor. When he is drunken, wants intense sexual relationship, which is quite painful. He hits and kicks her, even infront of the children. To avoid these circumstances, she lives separately in the same house. Her mother-in-law and husband live in another room. Despite this, her husband frequently abuses her. He is highly alcoholic and his habit has adversely affected the well-being of family members.

Abuses of Meera Gaur

Physical Abuses:	Hitting, kicking and throwing out, starring, no care to fulfill physical needs and necessities by husband.
Sexual Abuses:	Demand of excessive sexual relation, unusual ways of establishing sex-relation, embraces her infront of family members and neighbour by touching her organs etc.
Psychological Abuses:	Name calling, threatening of violence, non-cooperation, no emotional support, terrorizing.
Economic Abuses:	No financial support by husband, he is unemployed, doing nothing and forcefully snatches her earning (money) and spends it in liquor.
Consequences:	High feeling of stress, feeling of insecurity, very poor condition, scarcity and living hand to mouth, social isolation, feeling of helplessness.

Case XII (Amna)

Amna, a 30 year old housewife, married at an early age of 10 yrs. belongs to a muslim family. Her husband is a mechanic in a Rikshaw Company and lives with his family in Gorakhpur city. Amna has 5 children (2 daughters and 3 sons). Family income is insufficient for household needs because her husband takes liquor everyday. She is highly abused by her husband. He beats her every next day. When he comes back heavily drunken, starts beating her for no significant reasons like, complaining against children, neighbours, food etc. He blames her and says that she has extra marital affair. In fact, he wants excessive sex relations and even infront of others. If she refuses he starts beating and calls her 'prostitute'. He does not allow her to go anywhere even to the market. The lady has very poor health and is deprived of basic necessities.

Abuses of Amna

Physical Abuses:	Beating, slapping, throwing or kicking by her husband very frequently.
Psychological Abuses:	Name calling (prostitute), terrorizing and threatening, by husband.
Drug abuse and Sexual abuses:	Takes liquor everyday and at night starts harassing her sexually, exposure, excessive demand of sex even she is not physically well.
Consequences:	Highly stressed, feeling of helplessness and insecurity, social isolation, poor physical and mental health status, high incidence of child abuse (by husband).

4

Discussion

Findings of the present study are interpreted and discussed under five major sections. At the out set, major findings of the study have been interpreted in accordance with the statistical treatments. Further, the role of social and psychological variables in the origin and sustenance of domestic violence and its impact on behavioural functioning of children have been discussed in subsequent sections. More specifically, the first section deals with the pattern and trend of domestic violence in rural and urban settings and the role of environmental factors in the origin of domestic violence have also been discussed. The linkages between social factors i.e., social status, caste and community and occupational characteristics of victims and perpetrators (husband) and domestic violence have been discussed and interpreted in the second section. Third section of the chapter deals with the significance of some psychological factors, i.e., marital conflict, stress and women empowerment in the emergence and sustenance of domestic violence. Fourth section, of the chapter focuses on the impact of domestic violence on emergence of child abuse and behavioural problems in children.

Major Findings of the Study

In brief, the findings of this research evinced that the pattern and trend of domestic violence (abuses) varied in accordance with variations in settings, socio-demographic and psychological characteristics of the respondents and perpetrators. Present findings are reported in nutshell:

(a) Result revealed that various forms of domestic violence are found equally at high rate in both the rural and urban settings. However, Physical abuse was found more in urban females than their rural counterparts.

- The trend of D.V. was found almost similar in both settings. However, psychological abuse was reported at higher level in rural females whereas, the incidence of physical and sexual abuses was identified more in urban females.

(b) Demographic characteristics of females and perpetrators (Husband) i.e.; age, education; occupation and health status were also found associated with domestic violence. It was found that;

- Middle age women (40+) reported being more victims of domestic violence than those of younger women.
- Illiterate women were found more abused than highly educated women. The extent of D.V. also differed across health status of females. Women with poor health status were found more abused than women with normal and good health status.
- Similarly, husband's education, occupation and income were also found to be associated with domestic violence. It was found that;

(i) Illiterate husbands were found more abusive than educated husbands.
(ii) Domestic violence (wife battering etc.) was committed at high rate by low occupation status (Labour class) husband than business or service class counterparts.

- Low income group of husbands were also found more abusive than middle and high income groups.

Certain family characteristics were also found significant predictors of domestic violence. Results evinced that:

- Women belonging to nuclear families were found more abused than those of joint and extended families.
- The extent of domestic violence (abuses) was significantly higher in larger families as compared with small size families.
- Women having two or more daughters were found more abused than those of having sons (male issues) and single daughter.

(iii) Certain social characteristics were also found important predictors of domestic violence. The level and extent of abuses varied across socio-economic status, caste and community. More specifically, it was found that:

- Majority of women belonging to low S.E.S. were found high victims of domestic violence than middle and high S.E.S. counterparts;
- Domestic violence was identified at high rate among schedule caste women than those of other backward caste (OBC) and general caste females respectively; and
- Prevalence rate of domestic violence was found little more in Muslim community than Hindu community.

Interpretation of Correlation Results

Correlation results indicate that various forms of domestic violence were found to be negatively related with women's education, socio-economic status, caste, community and health status but were positively related with women's age, which suggest that with increasing women's education, socio-economic status, caste and health status, the levels of abuse decreased. However, positive relationship with age suggests that the incidence of abuse increased with increasing the age of women.

Apart from this, domestic violence was found to be negatively related with husband's education, occupation and income. Findings, thus suggest that with increasing levels of education, income and occupation status, husbands were found less abusive.

Certain family characteristics i.e., type and size of the family were also found to be negatively related with domestic violence.

(d) A close perusal of the results obtained on third objective of the study, revealed that certain psychological characteristics i.e. marital conflict, stress and women empowerment, exerted influence on domestic violence. More specifically, it was found that:

- Women who reported high level of marital conflict were also found highly abused than the females of low conflict group.
- Empowered women were found less abused than low empowered women.

Correlation results indicate positive relationship between marital conflict and domestic violence (abuses). Further, stress was found positively correlated with domestic violence, whereas, women empowerment was found to be negatively related with domestic violence.

(e) Likewise, results obtained on fourth objective, clearly demonstrate the positive linkage between domestic violence and child abuse.

- Results evince that exposed group of children were found highly abused and neglected than unexposed group of children. Findings, thus, suggest that (a) the exposure of D.V. causes high incidence rate of child abuse and neglect, and (b) Domestic violence was also found positively correlated with various forms of abuse and neglect.

(f) A close perusal of the results obtained on fifth objective of the study, evinced the impact of the exposure to domestic violence on various behavioural functioning of children.

A set of behaviours viz.; aggression, non-compliance, destructive behaviour, bullying, helping behaviour, social interaction, affection, discipline, reciprocal relationship, task involvement and study behaviour were studied as a function of exposure level of domestic violence, environmental setting and socio-economic status. Results for each unit of behaviour are discussed:

(I) Aggression: ANOVA results revealed that the level of aggression differed significantly among different groups. Urban children were found highly aggressive than their rural counterparts. Further, low S.E.S. children expressed high level of aggression than middle and high S.E.S. counterparts and children exposed to D.V. expressed significantly higher level of aggression than unexposed children.

(II) Non-Compliance: Different groups of children differed significantly on non-compliance. More specifically—non-compliance was found at higher level in urban than rural children. Similarly, low S.E.S. children expressed high level of non-compliance than middle and high S.E.S. children. Children exposed to D.V. have showed higher level of non-compliance than their unexposed counterparts.

(III) Destructive Behaviour: Different groups of children varied significantly on destructive behaviour. It was found that Rural children expressed more destructive behaviour than their urban counterparts. Exposed children showed more destructive behaviour than unexposed children. Low S.E.S. children displayed more destructive behaviour than high and middle S.E.S. children respectively. Destructive behaviour was found significantly more in children exposed to domestic violence than non-exposed children.

(IV) Bullying: Bullying in children differed across different groups of children. Further findings of domestic violence influenced the bullying behaviour in children. It was found that children of rural setting showed more bullying behaviour than urban children. Similarly, low S.E.S. children displayed higher level of bullying behaviour than middle and high S.E.S. group. Bullying behaviour was also found higher in exposed children than their unexposed counterparts.

(V) Pro-Social Behaviour: Findings of this study further revealed that domestic violence adversely influenced the expression of pro-social behaviours in children. It was found that rural children showed more helping behaviour than urban children. Middle class children showed greater helping behaviour than high and low S.E.S. children. Despite this, exposed children expressed low helping behaviour than their unexposed counterparts.

(VI) Social Interaction: The level of social interaction also varied across different groups. It was found that social interaction was superior in middle class than low and high S.E.S. children. However, residential setting and exposure of domestic violence did not exercise significant impact on social interaction.

(VII) Affection: It is also clear from the result that low S.E.S. children expressed low level of affection with peers than high and middle S.E.S. children.

(VIII) Discipline: It is also apparent from the result that rural children were found highly undisciplined than urban children. Discipline was found very poor in low S.E.S. children than high and middle S.E.S. children respectively. Similarly, exposed children were found highly undisciplined than unexposed children.

(IX) Reciprocal-Relationship: Reciprocal relationship of children was also influenced by exposure level, environmental setting and socio-economic status. Rural children have shown poor reciprocal relationship than their urban counterparts. Middle S.E.S. children have shown better reciprocal relationship than low and high S.E.S. Contrary to this, exposed children showed poor reciprocal relationship than unexposed children.

(X) Task Involvement: Task involvement in children also varied significantly across exposure level of D.V. The exposed group of children expressed poor level of task involvement than unexposed children. However, environmental setting and S.E.S. effects were non-significant.

(XI) Study Behaviour: The study behaviour in children also varied in accordance with exposure level, environmental setting and S.E.S. Children exposed to D.V., were found poor in study behaviour, than unexposed counterparts. Similarly, study behaviour was found lower in rural and low S.E.S. children than their urban and middle/high S.E.S. counterparts.

Apart from ANOVA results, correlations were also calculated to establish linkages between domestic violence and its behavioural consequences. Positive behaviours i.e. helping behaviour, social interaction, affection, task involvement have been found inversely related with D.V. whereas, negative behaviours i.e., aggression, non-compliance, destructive behaviour and bullying, were found positively correlated with domestic violence (values were positive but low).

Predictions of Child Abuse and Behaviours by Domestic Violence

The Step-Wise Multiple Regression Analysis (SMRA) results indicate the contributing role of domestic violence in the incidence of child abuse and behavioural problems in children.

(i) Prediction of Child Abuse by Various Forms of Domestic Violence

Domestic violence (psychological) contributed positively to child abuse as a whole. Similarly, child psychological abuse was predicted by domestic violence (physical). Further, child economic abuse was predicted by domestic violence as a whole. Child physical neglect was also predicted by domestic violence (psychological). Child emotional neglect was also predicted by domestic violence as a whole and child educational neglect was also predicted by domestic violence as a whole.

(ii) Prediction of Child Behaviour by Domestic Violence

Helping behaviour of children was negatively predicted by child abuse as a whole, child emotional neglect and domestic violence (physical). Social interaction was also inversely explained by domestic violence (physical). However, Non-Compliance was positively predicted by child economic abuse. Destructive behaviour was also positively predicted by child abuse as a whole. However, affection was negatively predicted by child abuse as a whole. Discipline was also negatively predicted by child abuse as a whole. Reciprocal relationship was also inversely predicted by child physical neglect. Similarly, Task involvement was also inversely predicted by child abuse and domestic violence (physical).

Present findings thus, evinced the contributing roles of socio-psychological factors in domestic violence which in turn exercised damaging impact on children's behaviour.

On the basis of findings of present study, certain issues have been raised

1. How far these findings are in consonance with the other research findings?
2. How and at what extent socio-demographic and psychological factors contributed to the domestic violence?
3. At what extent, the ill consequences of domestic violence on behavioural functioning are confirmed, and how far environmental setting, and socio-economic status influenced these behavioural functionings?
4. What are the patterns of linkages between predictors and incidence of domestic violence as well as between domestic violence and its consequences?

Therefore, an effort was made to discuss these issues in the light of findings of present research as well as other empirical and theoretical evidences.

EMPIRICAL AND THEORETICAL VALIDATION OF THE FINDINGS

1. Domestic Violence in Relation to Ecological Perspectives

The findings of present study evinced ecological variations on various forms of domestic violence. Numerous contextual factors exercised significant role in the origin of domestic violence. Phenomenon of domestic violence often occur across four ecological levels; individual level (ontogenetic), the family (the micro-system), the community (the eco-system) and the culture (the macro-system) in which both the person and family factors are embedded. These factors are nested ecologically to each other (Belsky, 1984). Present findings revealed that Domestic Violence is present at alarming threshold in both the rural and urban communities, in some or other forms, however, trend of violence differed in both communities. It is apparent from the result of this study that except physical abuse, no significant variation was found for other forms of abuses in rural and urban societies. However, the trend of violence differed in both communities. Urban women reported higher level of physical (20%) and sexual abuses (21%) than rural women (Physical 16%; Sexual 14%). Contrary to this greater number of rural women (55%) were found victims of psychological abuses than urban counterparts (44%), however, equal number of rural and urban (15%) women were found economically abused.

Present findings thus, suggest that females are abused by their husbands or in-laws at high rate in our society. 'Lancet', a medical journal in London published that 'violence by an intimate partner is a common experience world-wide, in all but one setting women were at far greater risk of D.V. Further, a survey by World Health Organization (2006) revealed that rural areas tend to have higher rates of abuse than cities but no area was immune (WHO, 2006). However, the present finding evinced that domestic violence is present at high rate in both the rural and urban societies, however, psychological abuse was found higher in rural community whereas, physical and sexual abuse were witnessed more in urban areas. Domestic violence is also found more in larger families than small size families (Sedlak & Broadhurst, 1996). This study also evinced that women of nuclear family, having larger number of children were found more victimized than their comparison groups. This result can be explained on the basis of 'Strain Theory' and 'Structural Characteristics of the Family' (Brinkerhops & Lupri, 1988).

2. The Role of Socio-Demographic Variables in Domestic Violence

(a) Women Characteristics: The demographic characteristics of women were also found directly associated with domestic violence. These results are interpreted in relation to other empirical evidences.

(i) Women's age: It is apparent from the result that middle age women were found more abused than those of younger age females. Other studies also confirm this finding (Sedlak & Broadhurst, 1996). Females living in poor economic and emotionally oppressive environment in the family, feel helpless and start seeking sympathy and support outside the family. According to United Nations (UN) Population Fund Report, as many as 70 per cent of married women in India between the age of 15-49 are victims of beating, rape or coerced sex. Other studies also confirm that middle age women lack social support and were found high victims of violence than early adult age females (Ghosh, 2004; Visaria, 1999).

(ii) Women's Education: Results also denoted negative association between women education and domestic violence. Illiterate/low educated women were found victims of domestic violence at high rate than highly educated females. Education makes women more aware of their rights and responsibilities. They can rationalize and actively cope episodes up with stressful circumstances and also protect themselves from the abusing episodes. NIS (National Incidence Study) findings also confirm that low education was found positively linked with high rate of domestic violence.

(iii) Health Status: Weak or unhealthy females were found more abused than normal health women. Due to the 'poor health of females, especially if health problem is chronic and incurable, husband feels high level of stress and anxiety; consequently, they start abusing their wives. Another reason is, that due to poor health or inability, weak females are unable to fulfill the demands and expectations of husband or other family members, and therefore, they are neglected and disliked by them, get no appreciation and acceptance by family member and ultimately become the victim of domestic violence.

(b) Perpetrator's (Husband) Demographic Characteristics and Domestic Violence

Present results revealed that several demographic characteristics of perpetrators (husband or in-laws) were found closely associated with domestic violence. Major findings are interpreted in the light of other empirical/theoretical evidences.

(i) Education: Findings showed an inverse relationship between education of husband and domestic violence. Illiterate or low educated husbands were found more abusive than highly educated counterparts.

Due to the lack of awareness and meanness in accepting female dignity, they display domineering behaviour and become more abusive towards their wife and children. Other research findings also confirmed the linkage of poor education level and violence (Flavia, 1988 Sedlak & Broadhurst, 1996).

(ii) Occupation: Results of the present study also revealed that low occupation status of husband (labour class) was found positively related with D.V. Labour class husbands were found more abusive than cultivators, businessmen and service class respectively. Reasons are obvious and can be explained on the basis of role of numerous socio-cultural and psychological variables. Due to their low economic status and unstable resources of income, labour class families are bound to live in hand to mouth. Excessive poverty, illiteracy, social isolation, poor social support and lack of responsibilities towards their family, orient them to commit abusive activities (domestic violence) (Kurtz *et al.*, 1993; Trickett *et al.*, 1991).

(iii) Income: It appears from the result that income level of husband was also found to be associated with domestic violence. All forms of abuses were found significantly higher in low income group than middle and high income counterparts. Contrary to this, substance abuse was found at high level in low income people. They spent major amount of their earnings to purchase liquor and being unable to fulfill bare necessities of households, become violent against wife and children. These results can be explained on the basis of 'Strain Theory' which suggests that high level of D.V. is witnessed in low income or unemployed families (Limber & Nation, 1998). As stress and frustration become excessive, husband's aggression may be directed to poor women (wife) and children.

(c) Family and Social Characteristics

(i) Caste and Community: Present results revealed that domestic violence was found at high rate in SC/ST families than other backward caste and upper caste families. Similarly, the incidence of domestic violence was identified at high rate in Muslim community as compared to Hindu community. Results are explained on the basis of socio-cultural factors. Communities who are economically or socially disadvantaged, or in minority, are sufferers of social isolation. Since social isolation is eventually a noted characteristic feature of abusive families, who lack social recognitions, adequate care, peer groups, close friends and adequate housing (Thompson, 1994). Abusive partners often lack social control on others in the family, neighbourhood, community and social agencies, which provide needed support and assistance (Korbin, 1994).

Numerous studies support that there are multiple factors responsible for high rate of violence in low status families. Coulten *et al.* (1995) identified that in low class families, unstable or violent family situation, (Straus, *et al.*, 1980), several disadvantages (Housing, privacy, noise, pollution, crowding etc.) are very common and emerge as major socio-cultural factors exercising impact on high rate of domestic violence. In a study it was found that in a village in Punjab 75 per cent of women from Scheduled Caste households reported victim of regular physical assault (Mahajan, 1990).

(ii) Socio-Economic Status: Present results also evinced that women of low SES families reported high victims of D.V. than middle and high SES families respectively. This finding is also supported on the basis of numerous other studies, conducted in India and abroad. As National Incidence Study (NIS III) reports, females of low income strata were significantly more victims of domestic violence, however, females of different strata were also found abused in some or other forms (Pandey, 2005).

It is essential to note that several factors associated with poverty, may contribute to domestic violence viz; poor residential setting, low education, high rate of substance abuse and emotional problems. Moreover, families with low socio-economic status have poor social support system to cognize husband and other family members for their responsibilities to care and regard with women in the family, community and society (Sedlak & Broadhurst, 1996). Salient demographic characteristics and their influence on domestic violence are interpreted and discussed in the light of findings of present study and other research evidences.

(iii) Family Structure: It is also identified in the present study that domestic violence was found higher in nuclear families than those of joint families.

Infact, nuclear and joint family structures include but different forms of several burdens, difficulties, and stressors. In nuclear families, wife and husband are over burdened in fulfilling domestic and professional activities, and also lack family support system. In case of double career families, it becomes more serious issue. Personal—professional interface causes high demands to fulfil a numerable number of activities. Person, unable to cope with such challenges feel high level of stress and sometimes becomes abusive against his wife or children. Other studies also evinced that females of nuclear families are found prone to high stress (Pandey & Srivastava,

2004), which is also found closely linked with domestic violence and child maltreatment (Korbin, 1987). This finding can also be explained on the basis of 'Strain theory'.

(iv) Family Size: Results of this study also indicated that females in larger families were found more abused than small size families. The crowd in larger family causes high feeling of stress in family members or conflict between husband and wife which in turn, orient them to commit abusive acts or domestic violence. This finding receives support from NIS research (Sedlak & Broadhurst, 1996) which reported that in larger families, females and children are three times more physically abused than smaller families. Since additional members in a family means excess responsibility and additional risk of physical or sexual violence by a partner than by other people.' The WHO report says that rural areas tend to have slightly higher rates of abuse than cities. But no area was found immune to domestic violence (World Health Organization Report, 2006). Results, thus confirm that low social status of family has direct link with high incidence of Domestic Violence.

3. The Role of Psychological Factors in Domestic Violence

Second objective of the study was to explore the associations between psychological variables and domestic violence. In present study, marital conflict, stress and empowerment level in women were investigated and their linkages with different forms of domestic violence were determined. Findings are interpreted below:

(i) Marital Conflict and Domestic Violence

Findings of present study evinced an exclusively positive relationship between marital conflict and domestic violence. Magnitude of relationship varied among abusive and non-abusive partners. It is apparent from the result that women facing high level of marital conflict also reported being victims of domestic violence. Other studies also support this finding. In one of the earliest studies of marriage, Terman, Buttenweiser, Ferguson, Johnson and Wilson (1938) reported that husbands' marital grievances were most likely to involve their wives' complaining, criticizing, and escalating emotion, whereas wives' grievances were most likely to involve their husbands' emotional withdrawal. Happily married couples have been found to display higher ratios of agreement to disagreement (Gottman, 1979) and exhibit more positive nonverbal cues (Birchler, 1977; Haynes, Follingstad & Sullivan, 1979), more agreement and approval (Vincent & Friedman, 1979) and less coercive and attacking behaviours (Billings, 1979) than unhappily married couples. In present study, a sizable number of women reported high level of marital conflict and dissatisfaction. They also reported complains of extra marital relation and regular physical sexual, psychological and economic abuses by husbands or in-laws.

(ii) Stress and Domestic Violence

In the present study, stress and domestic violence were found positively correlated to each other. Abused victims expressed high level of stress than non abused women. Other studies also confirm that abusive partners reported high level of stress than non-abusive counterparts (Gil, 1971; Korbin, 1994). The impact of any stressful event is substantially influenced by how a person appraises it. If family environment is extremely stressful and husband or family members are unable to cope with stressful episodes, negative outcome takes place.

In this study, stress was identified as a cause as well as outcome of the domestic violence. Despite the high level of stress in abusive husband (partner), abused females also expressed high level of stress than non-abused females. Since stressful events in the family affect females in different and unique ways. However, certain stressful situations trigger more intense stress reactions and consequences than others. In another study, Pandey (2005) observed that stress and frustration were the major causal factors of child abuse/ domestic violence. Apart from this, domestic violence is certainly one of the worst and most intrusive forms of stress (Korbin, 1994).

(iii) Buffering Role of Women Empowerment in Domestic Violence

Present results evinced an inverse relationship between empowerment and domestic violence. Various forms of abuses were found very high in de-empowered women whereas, empowered group of women reported a few incidences of domestic violence in the family. Results further revealed that domestic violence was mitigated by high level of empowerment in women. This result is also supported by other empirical evidences (Mahadevan, 2002).

Domestic Violence: A State of De-empowerment

Domestic violence or crime against women is considered a state of de-empowerment. Women and children (minors) have been victimized since a long period and therefore, this issue has become a primary impetus in stimulating the academicians, professionals and women organizations (Brown & Ziefert, 1988). Kahn and Behavioural Health Technician Staff (1980) identified numerous socio-cultural factors (patriarchy, family practices, dominance etc.) in the root of domestic violence. They reported that wife beating or domestic violence were a routine occurrence, stemmed from a view that women are men's property. Researchers found that abuses (beating) were interpreted as caring, they concluded that this practice can not be totally condemned since it would negate an important aspect of the communities culture. Studies indicate that women are still in a state of de-empowerment and facing blantalory discriminative practices resulting in the forms of physical, sexual, economic and psychological abuses. Review of a sizable number of studies indicates that in our society females are blamed to be responsible in varying degree of being abused (King, Rotter, Calhoun & Selby, 1978; Resick & Jackson, 1981). In another study, the victims of extreme age ranges (60+) were considered to be less responsible for victimization than those of middle age ranges (Colhoun *et al.*, 1980).

Coping with domestic violence or victimization is another category of studies related to women empowerment (Gordon & Bailly, 1982). Researchers have shown that protective behaviour (avoidance coping) develops dependency and docility and limits women's access to resources. Rosenberg (1985) evinced that women exposed to domestic violence in their childhood expressed avoidance coping styles and less active coping responses. Claerhout; Elder and Janes (1982) found that non battered and empowered women generated more alternatives when faced with violent situations. Mahadevan (2005) has emphasized to make women empowered. Through this process, they can achieve resourceful life with freedom, autonomy to choose her career, exercise active coping to confront with stressful episodes, freely decide to live healthy life style and can establish her free from all discriminations and inequalities.

A cursory glance at review of the present findings and other evidences revealed the significance of numerous social and psychological factors in the origin and prevalence of domestic violence in our society.

4. Impact of Domestic Violence on Children

The fourth and fifth objectives of the study were to investigate the impact of Domestic Violence (D.V.) on children. The consequences of D.V. were determined by:

(i) Establishing the linkages between domestic violence and child abuse; and
(ii) Investigating the behavioural functioning of children in relation to the exposure of D.V., residential setting and socio-economic status.

The findings, displayed in result section are discussed and interpreted on the basis of empirical evidences.

(i) Relationship Between Domestic Violence and Child Abuse

Present results revealed exclusively positive relationships between exposure of domestic violence and various forms of child abuse. Further, children who were exposed to domestic violence were found more victims of child abuse than non-exposed group of children. Stepwise multiple regression analysis also revealed that domestic violence contributed positively to the incidence of various forms of child abuse.

Findings can be interpreted on the basis of a numerable number of empirical evidences. Recent reviews of studies across different settings and with different samples indicate that the co-occurrence of child abuse and spousal abuse is found high. In an examination of nearly three dozen studies, reviewers found similar empirical findings: between 30 per cent and 60 per cent of children whose mothers had experienced abuse were themselves likely to be abused (Edleson, 1999). According to recent literature reviews, there are nearly one million children who were identified by child protection services as victims of substantiated or indicated abuse or neglect and well over one million American women who were physically assaulted within the past 12 months (Weithorn, 2001). Frequently, these women and children are in the same homes.

Over 30 studies of the link between these two forms of violence (D.V. and child abuse) show a 41 per cent median co-occurrence of child maltreatment and adult domestic violence in families studied (Holden *et al.,* 1998), with a wide range of findings depending on the sample explained (Edleson, 1999b). Since, family is the basic unit of children's socialization where children learn powerful strategies from their parents for resolving conflicts and to cope with unfavourable circumstances. However, children from abusive families may fail to learn how to moderate their emotions when they are exposed to their parent's anger and emotional outbursts (Cummings *et al.,* 1985). When children observe domestic violence committed by father against mother, they find them poor role model and may sometimes be victimized by parents or elder siblings. Straus *et al.* (1980) found that most batterers have themselves been exposed to their mothers' victimization in childhood. A sizable number of studies evince that children may be exposed to less severe and less frequent forms of spousal violence but be profoundly affected by the presence of other risk factors such as isolation, learning disabilities or self blaming. Sometimes, many children are injured either intentionally or accidentally during a violent episode (Jafe *et al.,* 2003, 2001). Present findings can be explained on the basis of Social Learning Theory (Bandura, 1991; 1994) and Attachment Theory (Bowlby, 1991) of Domestic Violence/Child Abuse.

(ii) Consequences of D.V. on Behavioural Functioning of Children

Present study also investigated the impact of D.V. on behavioural functioning of children. Results are interpreted below:

(i) Impact of Domestic Violence on Negative Behaviours: Results revealed positive associations between domestic violence and negative behaviours i.e., aggression, non-compliance, destructive behaviour and bullying in children. Abused children showed higher level of negative behaviours than unexposed children. The level of aggression, non-compliance, destructive behaviour and bullying was also high in urban and low S.E.S. children than their rural and middle/high S.E.S. counterparts. Correlation results revealed positive linkages between domestic violence and negative behaviours. In other words, with increasing the exposure of intense maltreatments of mother, aggression against father (perpetrator) also increases dramatically at high rate in children.

This result has sound support from a sizable number of empirical and theoretical evidences. Aggression is one of the most widely studied area of the outcome of domestic violence. A bulk of studies conducted worldwide, confirms the heightened aggression and related externalizing behaviours in children who are exposed to or direct victims of physical abuse (National Academy of Sciences, 1993; Shields, Cicchetti & Ryan, 1994; Wolfe *et al.,* 1998). High aggression and other problems in abused children may be related to the witnessing family violence and other negative life events. High level of family conflicts, including verbal and physical aggression has been found to be associated with emotional problems and diminished social functioning (Fantuzzo *et al.,* 1991). Pandey

(2005) showed positive association between poor family environment, child abuse and aggressive behaviour in children. In another study, Pandey (2004-a) showed heightened level of aggression in abused children, particularly belonging to low S.E.S. group.

(ii) Consequences on Positive Behaviours: Findings of the study revealed an inverse association between domestic violence and positive behaviours viz. pro-social behaviour, social interaction, discipline affection, reciprocal relationship, task involvement and study behaviour. ANOVA results denoted that exposed and low S.E.S. children exhibited less positive behaviours than unexposed, middle/high S.E.S. children respectively.

Since behaviours in children are determined by numerous personal, social and situational factors and abusive families provide poor model to imitate positive behaviours. Consequently, abused children express low level of these behaviours. Some studies have shown that children who witness domestic violence may be hampered in their social and school development (Moore, Pepler, Mae & Michele, 1989; Randolf & Talamo, 1997). Children who have been exposed to violence may be preoccupied with this issue and have difficulty in concentrating on school work. Their social development may be hampered because they are too sad, anxious or preoccupied to participate in social activities.

A sizable number of studies indicated numerous social difficulties, including deficits in pro-social behaviour, as a result of domestic violence. Results also revealed that urban children exposed to D.V. were found less helping than their rural unexposed counterparts city/urban life is more taxing in terms of time, cost and effort. Urban people suffer from information overload and stress related to daily life hassles. Hence, they lack interaction and behave less pro-socially than rural people. Similarly, children exposed to D.V. display deficiency in pro-social behaviour and communication and show more negative behaviours. They also showed disturbed peer interaction, deficits in pro-social behaviour, social withdrawal and isolation (Crittenden, 1992; Holfman-Plotkin & Twentyman, 1984; Prino & Peyrot, 1994).

Findings thus, confirm that several social (contextual, familial) and psychological factors determine the frequency and intensity of domestic violence which in turn exercise adverse impact on behavioural functioning of children.

THEORETICAL PERSPECTIVES OF DOMESTIC VIOLENCE

Domestic violence has been conceptualized as a social-psychological phenomenon nested in the ongoing interactions of family members, social and cultural variables embedded with each other. To analyze the family violence in general and domestic violence in particular, numerous macro level (sociological) and micro level (psychological) theories have been developed. An effort has been made to analyze the findings of present study in the light of these social and psychological perspectives.

1. Sociological Perspectives

The findings of the present study are in consonance with the theoretical explanations given by many macro level perspectives viz., Feminist theory, cultural explanations, structural characteristics of the family, strain theory, social bonding and deterrence theory.

(I) Feminist Theory

This theory identifies the roots of violence in a patriarchal society wherein women's inequality and society's tolerance of male violence is common place—especially in the context of intimate relationships. Within these relationships, men have historically been given the right to punish or discipline their partners as harshly as they seem appropriate (Dobash & Dobash, 1992). Many feminists do not approve of the term "family violence" because it removes a gender analysis from the discussion. A phrase such as "violence against women and children" is considered, by feminists, a more accurate descriptor of the reality of violence experienced within the home (Kane, 2000).

There is agreement between feminists and non-feminists that women are more likely to be victims of violence within their intimate relationships; both groups recognize that men may also be victims of violence, but women are found ten times more abused victims than male counterparts throughout the world. Other sociological theories also explain the causative roots of D.V. in society.

(II) The Structural Characteristics of the Family

Present study also revealed that family structure and other characteristics of the family were also found closely linked with domestic violence. Family structure sometimes makes individuals/families prone to violence (Brinkerhoff & Lupri, 1988). The negative pattern of interaction with family members, which causes tension and emotional insecurity, and such insecurities make family relationship volatile. Another factor is the power differential between family members. Since female have inferior status in the family and so they often become target of violence. The privacy of family also facilitate the occurrence of domestic violence by making violence relatively easy to hide and provide autonomy in deciding how to have control on women. Present study also evinced that incidence of domestic violence was found at higher rate in nuclear families because women in such family structure lack support system and privacy in the family facilitates male member (husband/father-in-law) to commit violence against women.

(III) Control Theory

The findings of present study are also supported by the Deterrence theory (Gibbs, 1975), also known as 'Control theory', which focuses on the influence of formal social controls. Gelles and Straus (1988) suggest that husbands abuse their wives when there are insufficient legal structure to keep from loosing control over wife or family members. Straus *et al.* (1980)

have mentioned in their book, that Domestic violence often takes place "Behind Closed Doors", where physical separation from society and family privacy provide husband's considerable autonomy. Therefore the cultural acceptances of husband to wife abuses blur the line between legitimate discipline and domestic violence.

(IV) Social Bonding Theory

Another finding of present study is that family with certain demographic and socio-psychological characteristics were found highly abusive and this result can be explained on the basis of "Social Bonding theory". The theory attempts to answer the questions that in a given cultural and social context, which factors encourage family violence? Why some people are more violent them others? Since, social bonding theory proposes that most people are sufficiently motivated to commit deviant act. (Domestic Violence) Yet what social forces prevent certain people from committing abusive acts ? People do not commit deviant acts when they have a stake in conformity. Three components of social bonds viz.; lack of commitment, attachment and belief determine the probability of domestic violence. Numerous studies on domestic violence are in consonance with social bonding theory. Young husband typically have less at stake conformity along with higher rates of domestic violence. Social and economic status also contribute to domestic violence through its impact on social integration (attachment bond). Families which are highly involved in the community life are less likely to be abusive. Husbands/families who lack important attachment have less at stake in conformity and therefore, more likely to be abusive. Similarly, families with positive views of the community and active in community are less likely to be violent (Garbarino & Kostelny, 1992).

(V) Cultural Perspective

Present results revealed that domestic violence was found at alarming volume in all strata of society. This finding can be interpreted on the basis of cultural explanation/perspective, which suggests that violence is an accepted and encouraged form of cultural expression in our society. The acceptance of violence in the culture contributes to high violence rates in the family or in the society (Straus, 1977; Tolan & Guerra, 1998). The aggression and violence in home reflects the societies' tolerance for aggression (Wyatt, 1994). Apart from this, the family norms also influence at certain extent of family aggression. Control in the name of family norms, is the cost and implantation of cost that men and other family members impose on women can vary from physical assault to psychological abuses and costs also range from legitimate to illegitimate dimensions. The findings of this study can be very well interpreted on the basis of cultural explanations.

(VI) Strain Theory

Present study also evinced that domestic violence was found maximum in women of low caste (SC/ST), low socio-economic status and low occupation status families. Present findings receive support from "Strain Theory", which suggests that high rate of domestic violence is found in low income families, unemployed families and family receiving aids or benefits (Limber & Nation, 1998) the unequal distribution of opportunities along with the stressors associated with poverty (financial worries, ill health and crowded living conditions) produced high level of stress and frustration in lower income families (Farrington, 1980; Straus, 1980). As stress and frustration become overwhelming husband's aggression may be directed to poor women. The structure of velocity theory suggests that the lower class violence to some extent, is a cultural norm, a way of life (Wolfgang & Ferraculti, 1972).

2. Psychological Perspectives

Although, sociological theories successfully explain why domestic violence exists in a society but they fail to explain why individual family members are violent ? Primarily, these theories interpret domestic violence in structural terms, but do not explain variations in individual's cognitions, motivations and action tendencies. Explaining the action or behaviour of individuals, is more difficult than explaining structural pattern of violence, hence certain psychological theories have endeavoured to identify risk factors that make domestic violence more understandable and predictable. Thus, interpretation of present results in relation to psychological perspectives has been done in this section.

(i) Psychopathology

One popular explanation of domestic violence is that mentally disturbed individuals commit more abusive or deviant acts (Kempe, *et al.*, 1962). Hunter *et al.* (1990) reported that higher rates of psychological disorders were found in offenders of domestic violence. However, some researchers argue that psychopathology is found only in the few individuals who physically or sexually abused their wives or children (Straus, 2000; Milner, 1998; Williams & Finkelhor, 1990).

(ii) Biological Factors

Present results and other studies also support that biological factors of abusers were found to be associated with domestic violence. Abusers show hyper-responsive physiological activity to both the positive and negative stimuli concerning women or children. Such activity might make the abuser more physiologically reactive in stressful situation with women and children and lead to violence (Milner & Chilamkurti, 1991). Other biological factors i.e. I.Q., neuropsychological deficiencies, deficit disorders, physical disabilities and disorder and health problems were found closely linked with domestic violence/child abuse (Crittenden, 1992; Milner, 1998; Pandey, 2004, 2007).

(iii) Psychological Characteristics

Findings of the present study evinced that abusive husband and abused victim (wife) expressed high levels of stress and marital conflicts. Other researchers have also identified that abusive husband or family members showed higher level of cognitive distortions, depressive symptoms, stress, low self esteem, more substance abuse or dependence as compared with non-abusive members (Chan, 1994; Ethier *et al.*, 1995; Milner *et al.* 1995). Certain other studies reported that abusive husbands display more anger control problems, hostility and low frustration tolerance than non-abusive husbands (Bauer & Twentyman, 1985; Milner *et al.*, 1995). It appears that certain psychological and behavioural factors jointly lead to occurrence of domestic violence.

(iv) Interaction Theorys

Results of the present study are also confirmed with the reciprocal nature of the husband-wife relationship. This theory suggests that poor bond between husband and wife or poor relationship with husband or in-laws are resulted in the form of domestic violence. Abusive families are characterized by disturbed patterns of attachments (Kolko, 1992). The 'Attachment theory' (Bowlby, 1980) suggests that attachment is an enduring emotional bond that develops during the early years of marital life and failure to form a secure attachment in early life may contribute to problems in the form of inability to develop belief and close personal relationship with each other (Ainsworth & Bowlby, 1991; Frankel & Bates, 1990). The insecure pattern of attachment causes high level of domestic violence against women and children (Crittenden, 1998; Pandey, 2005). Researchers have also pointed out that insecure attachments are caused by behavioural unresponsiveness to the physical and psychological needs for the women. Poor bond between husband and wife may lead to abusive husband and abused wife relations (Cerezo, 1997; Crittenden, 1998; Hurlock, 1984).

(v) Social Learning Theory

The impact on domestic violence on children was also investigated in this study. Results revealed the negative consequences of exposure to domestic violence on occurrences of child abuse and behavioural problems in children. These findings can be successfully analyzed on the basis of Bandura's Social Learning Theory (1991). He emphasized the process of modeling in which individual learns social behaviour by simply observing and imitating model's behaviour. Children exposed to violence directly or indirectly learn with the set of norms and rationalization that justify violence. They acquire that violence is an acceptable way of resolving family conflicts and expressing emotions. Thus, observation and reinforcement of violence within a social context teach them how to perform abusive act.

The application of this theory has achieved empirical validation on several points. First violence tends to perpetrate itself from one generation to next, "like father like son" "like mother like daughter" (Straus *et al.*, 1980). Secondly, numerous studies with school children evinced that aggression can be learned through modeling (Bandura, Ross and Ross, 1961). Lastly, sizable number of studies have linked the exposure to violence in childhood to violence in adulthood (Widom, 1989; Williams & Finkelhon, 1990). Although inter-generational patterns of domestic violence is criticized and requires further empirical validations (Kaufman & Zigler, 1987; Widom, 1989).

Further Evaluation of the Theoretical Status of Domestic Violence

In the light of present study and other researches, some issues have been raised, which are still unresolved in these theories. The macro level sociological theories explain very well the structural roots of domestic violence. The cultural explanations focus on broad cultural forces that may promote abusive activities whereas, structural characteristics of the family suggest the contributing role of family dynamics in domestic violence. Similarly, sociological theories of deviance applied to explain domestic violence are ; Strain theory, Social bonding theory and Deterrence theory. Although, the sociological theories successfully discuss why domestic violence exists in a society or why some segment of society experience more violence than others but they fail to explain the process involved in the origin, occurrence, maintenance and consequences of domestic violence. Since explaining the process of abusive behaviour is more complex than explaining structural patterns, consequently the answer becomes difficult. Further, macro-level theories cannot properly explain why some adults (husband) abuse their wife more and others do not? And therefore, it becomes difficult to predict who will be violent?

Thus, micro-level psychological theories viz; psychopathology, personality traits, biological factors, social learning theories and interactional theories have been applied to explain the psychological processes involved in abusive (violent) behaviours. However, biological, psychopathological and personality traits mainly emphasize the causes of problem within the person (perpetrator), whereas the social learning theory and the interaction theories focus on roles of context, family, and social agents in the process of domestic violence.

Despite this, there is a need to develop a wide range theory of domestic violence which can better explain the complex nature of domestic violence, numerous causative factors and process of domestic violence which can better respond to issues viz., what is domestic violence? How is domestic violence and why is domestic violence? To answer these questions, it is essential to explore the role of genetic factors along with the mediating processes in between the antecedents and consequences of domestic violence.

5

Conclusion and Recommendations

Conclusion

This research study endeavoured to investigate the Psycho-Social dynamics of domestic violence and its impact on children. Present piece of work is not merely a theoretical exercise, but is also based on household empirical data from a large segment of rural and urban population belonging to different strata of society.

(i) The findings of present study indicate the role of salient social and psychological variables in the origin and sustenance of D.V. in our society. Present results revealed that violence behind closed doors (D.V.) is present at alarming threshold in both the rural and urban settings with little variations in its pattern and trends. However, the incidence rate of domestic violence is identified significantly high in the families with low socio economic status, occupation, low caste (SC/ST) and Muslim community. Apart from this; age, education and health status of perpetrators (Husband) and victims (wife or children) also contributed significantly to domestic violence. Illiteracy, young or middle age of respondents and poor health or disability lead to high incidence of violence against women. Similarly, illiterate, alcoholic or drug addict and low status husband were found more abusive. Further more, family structure and family size also played significant role; respondents belonging to nuclear families and having more number of children were found victims of domestic violence than their comparison groups.

(ii) Apart from socio-demographic characteristics of perpetrators, victims and the family, certain psychological factors viz; marital conflict, life stress and women empowerment also played significant role in the occurrence of D.V. Present finding denotes that high conflict in marital relationship caused various forms of abuses against women at high rate. Similarly, high level of stress in husband and wife also favourably contributed to high incidence of D.V. Contrary to this, women empowerment exercised buffering impact on mitigating the incidence of domestic violence and its consequences. De-empowered women reported high incidence of domestic violence than their empowered counterparts.

(iii) Another significant finding of this study is that exposure of domestic violence caused serious impact on children. Result revealed an exclusively positive relationship between various forms of domestic violence and child abuse. Children exposed to domestic violence were also found highly abused than their non exposed counterparts.

(iv) The exposure of domestic violence also created behavioural problems in abused children of low strata. These children displayed heightened aggression, non-compliance, destructive behaviour and bullying activities. Despite this, exposed children showed low helping behaviour, poor reciprocal relationship, affection, poor social interaction and indiscipline. These children were also found inferior in task involvement and study behaviour.

Present study, therefore, evinced that the practice of domestic violence is not only damaging the dignity, health and well-being of women community but also ruining the overall development of children. The findings of present study have

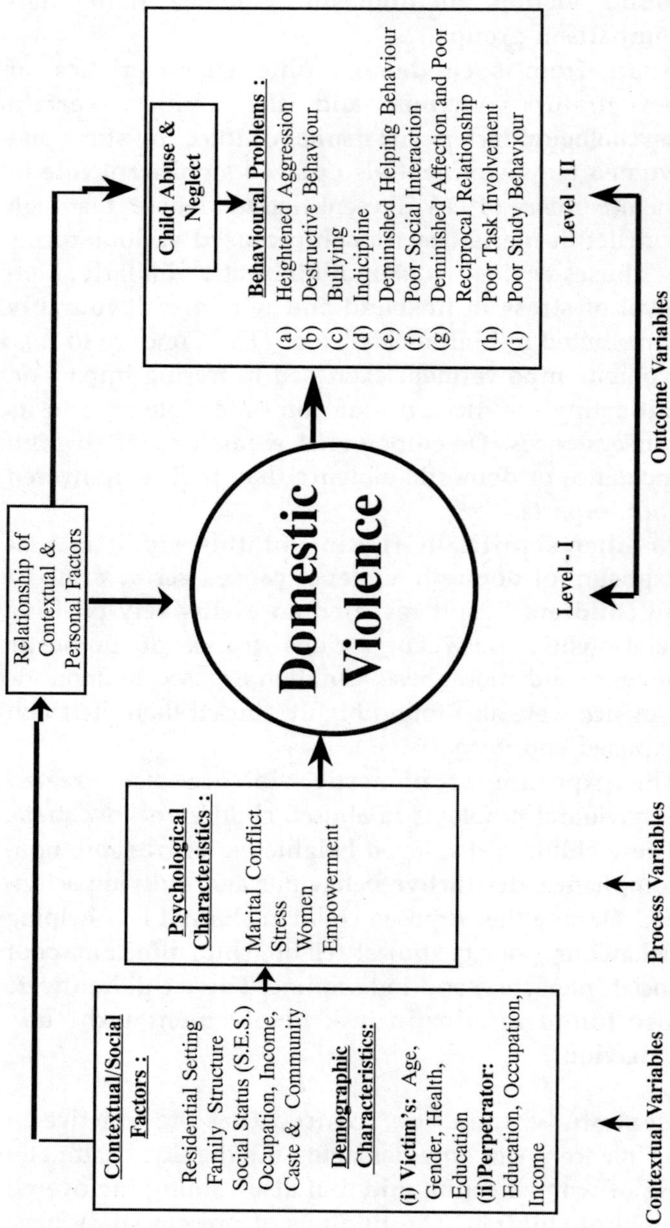

Fig 5.1: Psycho-Social Dynamics of Domestic Violence and Its Consequences

been integrated in the model (Fig. 5.1), developed by present researcher, emphasizing the linkages between antecedent factors, mediating processes and consequences of domestic violence.

Researcher asserts that women and children should be viewed as the most vulnerable/high risk group of population and they need urgent preventive and promotive interventions at multiple points and ecological settings. Therefore, study proves its theoretical and practical significance.

On the basis of findings of the present study, tentative recommendations are given below:

Recommendations

A cursory glance at findings of present study reveals that domestic violence is epidemic in our society. A large segment of women community is in the direct trap of this evil and therefore, it is urgently required to chalk out intervention programmes combining both reactive (short-term) and proactive (long term) strategies to root out this evil from our society.

The short term strategies include: crisis intervention, social support, bystander intervention, legal support etc. Whereas, proactive responses to domestic violence involves: Generating awareness, changing socialization pattern and child rearing practices, empowering women educationally, financially and politically, raising public consciousness, organizing women's help group, providing counseling and consultation to cope with stressful episodes, education for positive parenting and gender sensitization etc. These efforts will be instrumental to promote the status of abused victims in particular and women community in general. Thus, following preventive intervention devices should be exercised:

1. Develop Systematic Understanding of the Ingredients of Domestic Violence

Prior to designing any intervention programme, it is essential to systematically scrutinize the causative roots of domestic violence from multidimensional approaches. Belsky (1980) has proposed four ecological roots of domestic violence/abuses viz; at ontogenetic level (personal factors), micro system (family factors), macro system (social factors) and exo-system (cultural factors) levels respectively. Based on Belsky model numerous preventive programmes have been developed and implemented at national and international levels. However, the graph of abusers and abused victims is increasing dramatically. So it is suggested to plan innovative and imaginative intervention strategies to counteract the prevalence of domestic violence in our society.

2. Generate Knowledge Through Awareness Programme

Present results suggest sensitizing the public and disadvantaged community about issues related to women rights and domestic violence. Public should be made aware of pervasive legal efforts to protect women from domestic violence or any other crimes. The knowledge of Domestic Violence Prevention Act, 2005 and other legal effort to save victims should be extended (diffused) through strong networking between local community leaders, Government agencies, and Non-Government Organizations (NGOs). Workshops, conferences, meetings, role play and various communication channels should be exercised to cognize public, disadvantaged community and the victim (in particular) of domestic violence.

3. Promote Women Empowerment and Gender Equality

Present study indicated that a numerable number of women are de-empowered in the family, community and at the work place. They face blantatory discriminatory practices and are deprived of sharing equal opportunity in decision making. So, it is essential to design and implement intervention strategies to empower women economically, educationally, socially and politically. Simultaneously, public should be sensitized towards gender equality, human rights, and non-violence. Such efforts will be instrumental in making women empowered and healthy.

4. Prevent Health Hazards in Abused Victims

In present study, it was witnessed that a sizable number of abused victims reported poor health status and emotional disorders i.e., depression, anxiety and stress reactions. However, in the study setting, no adequate medical facility and counseling centers were observed. Community people were also found either ignorant or ill informed about the roots of emotional problems and linkages between physical and mental health. Thus, they should be correctly informed about the link of domestic violence, emotional trauma and health hazards through education programme. In addition, concerted efforts should be made by community psychologists, family counselors, health professionals and community leaders, to contact the family and male members (husband or in-laws) who are violent and encourage them to participate in the whole process which will help them to gain better knowledge and insight and this will in turn be relevant to change the attitude of these people in the positive direction. Further, intervention programme must integrate comprehensive medical and psychological care for abused victims. These efforts will be relevant in rebuilding and maintaining health and well-being of women and children.

5. Address Domestic Violence through Education

The findings of present study also suggest the essence of education programme to change the norms of society regarding violence as a controlling device. Since gender inequality and patriarchy are deep rooted concepts in our familial system developed through the course of social evolution. Thus, the concept of gender equality and human rights should be introduced in the socialization process and in education system. Women should also be educated on these issues through adult education programme.

6. Implement Programmes for Abused Children/Children Exposed to Domestic Violence

Present study also revealed a positive linkage between domestic violence and child abuse. Furthermore, children exposed to domestic violence showed serious behavioural problems. So, intervention programme should be designed for abused children or those who are exposed to domestic violence to modify their behaviour in positive direction. Apart from this, their parents should be made aware of the damaging consequences of domestic violence on overall development of their children. Parents should be given 'parenting training' for positive parenting style, stress management and effective coping style.

7. Generate Crisis Intervention Services

It was also witnessed in the study setting that domestic violence has achieved epidemic threshold in our society and abused victims showed acute fear and the feeling of learned helplessness (Seligman, 1975). Thus, it is suggested to generate crisis referral services or local hot line services in community setting so that woman or bystander can take calls from women organization or can consult for legal, medical or psychological services. Such services will serve victims who are socially and geographically at distant place.

8. Raise Social Support Network Social

Social support network has pervasive impact to check the incidence of domestic violence. Present study and other researches evince that social support has significant role in minimizing the prevalence rate of Domestic Violence. Such supports are provided by women help group, family counselors and neighbours of the victim. In a study, women organization (57%), community leaders, relatives and students in the role of para professionals and human right groups (41%) played important role in giving support to victims (Pandey & Mishra, 2000). Such efforts create public awareness of domestic violence and how to save victims from such incidents. Sometimes, informal groups (bystanders) play prominent role as compared to media in activating personal risk of victimization and effort to avoid such victimization.

9. Exercise Bystander Intervention

The role of 'Bystanders' in the prevention of D.V. can hardly be denied. They are treated as "eye to ears" of the police, for such purposes immediate neighbours, friends, relatives, other family members and local residents can serve as bystanders and can help to save victims from crimes. Sometimes these people ignore to intervene at very early stage considering it as other person's most personal matter, which later on lead to serious forms of crimes behind the closed doors. Despite this, public should be sensitized to take initiative and those who intervene should be rewarded and appreciated by the society and Government organizations.

10. Continue Communication with Global Support System

To check the incidence and prevalence rate of Domestic Violence, global efforts are essential. Thus, appropriate responses to D.V. should occur from local level (Community or setting) to Government level. Voluntary agencies should also be added with macro level intervention programme. The needs of the disadvantaged group (poor, low socio economic status, and minority group) should be kept in the main focus of programme. This combined effort will help to eradicate this evil from our society.

Right since the young age, a girl child should be made to speak against the wrong behaviour meted-out towards her, so that she may be able to grow up with confidence and self-respect. Parents should teach their female child to fight against the injustice and make her aware of the rights (both legal and social) provided to her by the system. This may help her in growing into a self-reliant individual, who may not only take care of her own self but also help other women in need.

11. Strengthen Legal Support System

Looking at the high increasing graph of Domestic Violence, Govt. of India has taken many steps to eradicate the evil of D.V. In this regard several Acts, Bills have been passed but contrary to expectation, the incidence of domestic violence has increased. A brief account of these Acts/Bills is given below. In order to check the incidence rate of domestic violence at national and international levels, numerous legal efforts have been made. Earlier IPC i.e., the Code of Criminal Procedure, 1973 and the Evidence Act 1972 were amended to deal effectively not only the cases of dowry deaths but also the cases of domestic violence. Further, Vienna accord of 1994, the Beijing Declaration and the Platform for Action 1995 declared that D.V. is a human rights issue and serious deterrent development of society. Further, The United Nations Committee on Convention of Elimination of All forms of Discrimination Against Women (CEDAW) has recommended that State parties should act to protect women against violence of any kind. Recently, on 13th September, 2005, 'The Protection of Women from Domestic Violence Act' has been placed by Govt. of India (Act No. 43 of 2005) to provide more effective protection of the rights of women, who are victims of any forms occurring within the family. Despite the worldwide consciousness and legal efforts to prevent domestic violence, the number of abusers and abused victims is still increasing day by day. Thus, it is suggested to cognize public, particularly disadvantaged community or rural people about the details of the Act (PWDVA) 2005 and Bills to protect women from various forms of crime and discriminations.

12. Reconceptualize Domestic Violence and Develop Innovative Research Strategy

Since domestic violence is considered an universal psycho-social phenomenon, however the nature and forms of abuse vary from culture to culture. This problem is extensively studied in western countries and therefore, the conceptualization of domestic violence is primarily made by western researchers, where prevention efforts are proliferated since the last few decades. Although some forms of abuses are common throughout the world, however some forms of abuses are culture specific. Thus, there is a need to reconceptualize and make a more comprehensive definition emphasizing contextual and cross-cultural perspectives. The conceptualization of domestic violence should also be done in a more Indianized manner. Apart from this, a wide range theory of domestic violence should be propounded. Despite this innovative, imaginative, community based and social action oriented research strategies should be developed to study the multifaceted dynamics of domestic violence and its damaging consequences. More specifically, the intervention programmes should be developed targeting the needs of the victims, keeping in view the socio-economic status and literacy levels of both the males (Perpetrators) and females (victims). Regular follow ups of intervention programmes and evaluation researches should be applied to access success of the programme. It is also essential to bridge the gap between academic and professional roles. This Holistic approach will be instrumental to prevent the incidence and prevalence rates of domestic violence in Indian society.

References

Ainsworth, M.D.S., & Bowlby, J. (1991). An ethological approach to personality development. *American Psychologist*, 331-341.

American Medical Association (1992). Violence against women. *Journal of the American Medical Association*, 267, 107-112.

American Psychiatric Association (2000). *Diagnostic and Statistical Manual of Mental Disorders* (DSM-IV-TR). Washington, DC: American Psychological Association.

Asthana, H. S. (1985). The concept of stress: Phenomenological approach. *Social Science International*, 1, 39-44.

Baig, T.A. (1976). *Indian's Woman Power*. New Delhi: S. Chand & Co.

Bandura, A. (1971). *Social Learning Theory*: Morris Town, NJ; General Learning.

Barton, K., & Dreger, R.M. (1986). Prediction of marital roles from normal and pathological dimensions of psychology: 16 PF and MMPI. *Psychological Reports*, 59, 459-468.

Baur, W.D., & Twentyman, C.T. (1985). Abusing, neglectful, and comparison mothers' responses to child-related and non-child related stressors. *Journal of Consulting and Clinical Psychology*, 53, 335-343.

Beach, S.R.H., Arias, I., & O'Leary, K.D. (1986). The relationship of marital satisfaction and social support to depressive symptomatology. *Journal of Psychopathology and Behaviour Assessment*, 8, 305-316.

Belsky, J. (1984). The determinants of parenting: A process model. *Child Development*, 55, 83-96.

Bem, S. (1974). The measurement of psychology androgyny. *Journal of Consulting and Clinical Psychology*, 42, pp. 155-62.

Berry, J.W. (1976). *Human ecology and cognitive style*, N.Y., Wiley.

Bhattacharya, R. (2004). *Behind closed doors: Domestic violence in India*. New Delhi: Sage.

Billings, A. (1979). Conflict resolution in distressed and non-distressed couples. *Journal of Consulting and Clinical Psychology*, 47, 368-376.

Birchler, G. (1977). A multi-method analysis of distressed and non-distressed marital interaction: A Social learning approach. *Paper Presented at the Meeting of the Western Psychological Association*, Seattle, WA.

Bowlby, J. (1980). *Attachment and loss: Vol. 3, Loss, Sadness, and Depression,* New York: Basic Books.

Brinkerhops, M.B., & Lupri, E. (1988). Interpersonal violence. *Canadian Journal of Sociology*, 13, 407-434.

Bronfenbrenner, U. (1977). Towards an experimental ecology of human development. *American Psychologist*, 32, 513-531.

Bronfenbrenner, U. (1979). *The Ecology of human development: Experiments by nature and design*. Cambridge, M.A.: Harvard University Press.

Brooks-Gunn, J. & Duncan, G. J. (1997). *The effects of poverty on children.: The Future of Children,* 7,(2) 55-71.

Brown, K., & Ziefert, M. (1988). Crisis resolution, competence, and empowerment: A service model for women. *Journal of Primary Prevention*, 1, 92-103.

Burgess, E.W., Locke, H.J., & Thomes, M.M. (1971). *The family*. New York: Van Nostrand Reinhold.

Calfee, R.C. (1975). *Human experimental psychology*. N.Y.: Holt.

Carlson, B.E. (1991). Emotionally disturbed children's beliefs and punishment. *Child Abuse and Neglect*, 15, 19-28.

Cartwright, S., & Cooper, C.L. (1994). *Meagers and acquisition: The Human Factor*, Oxford: Butter Warth Heinemann.

Cartwright, S., Cooper, C.L., & Barron, A. (1993). Manager stress and road accidents. *Journal of General Management*, 19(2), 78-85.

Cerezo, M.A. (1997). Abusive family interaction: A review. *Aggression and Violent Behaviour*, 2(3), 215-240.

Chan, Y.C. (1994). Parenting stress and social support of mothers who physically abuse their children in Hong-Kong. *Child Abuse and Neglect*, 18, 261-269.

Claerhout, S., Elder, J. & Janes, C. (1982). Problem-solving skills of rural battered women. *American Journal of Community Psychology*, 10, 605-612.

Coohey, C. (1996). Child Maltreatment: Testing the social isolation hypothesis. *Child Abuse and Neglect*, 20, 241-254.

Coulton, C.J., Korbin, J.E., Su, M. & Chow, J. (1995). Community level factors and child maltreatment rates. *Child Development*, 66, 1262-1276.

Cox, C., & Cooper, C.L. (1988). *High fliers: An anatomy of managerial success*. New York: Blackwell.

Cox, T. & Mackay, C. (1981). *A Transactional approach to occupation stress*. In E.N., Carlett, and J. Richardson (Eds), Stress, Work design and productivety. London: John Willey.

Crittenden, P.M. (1992). Children's strategies for coping with adverse home environments: An interpretation using attachment theory. *Child Abuse and Neglect*, 16(3), 329-339.

Crittenden, P.M. (1998). Dangerous behaviour and dangerous context: A 35-year perspective on research on the development effect of child physical abuse. In P. K. Trickett, and C.J. Schelienback (Eds.). *Violence against children in the family and the community* (pp. 11-38). Washington, D.C., American Psychological Association.

Cummings, E.M., Jannotti, R., & Zahn-Waxler, C. (1985). Influence of conflict between adults on the emotions and aggression of young children. *Developmental Psychology*, 21, 495-507.

D'Amato, M.R. (1970). *Experimental Psychology*, N.Y. McGraw Hill.

De Souza, A. (1975). *Women in contemporary India,* New Delhi: Manohar Publications.

Dobash, R.P., Dobash, R.E., Wilson, M., & Daly, M. (1992). The myth of sexual symmetry in marital violence. *Social Problems*, 39, 71-91.

Dumas, J., & Walher, R.G. (1985). Indiscriminate mothering as a contextual factor in aggressive—oppositional relationship. *Child Psychology*, 13, 1-17.

Edleson, J.L. (1999). The overlap between child maltreatment and woman battering. *Violence Against Women*, 5, 134-154.

Edleson, J.L., Eisikovits, Z.C., Guttmann, E., & Sela-Amit, M. (1991). Cognitive and interpersonal factors in woman abuse. *Journal of Family Violence*, 6, 167-182.

Egeland, B., Breitenbucher, M., & Rosenberg, D. (1980). Prospective study of the significance of life stress in the etiology of child abuse. *Journal of Consulting and Clinical Psychology*, 48, 195-205.

Eggeman, Moxley, & Schumm (1985). *Kansas Marital Conflict Scale*. In K.Corcoran & J. Fischer. (Eds.) Measures for clinical Practice: A source book (Vol. 1) New York. NY: Free Press.

Emery, R.E. (1982). Inter-parental conflict and the child of disorder and divorce. *Psychological Bulletin*, 92, 310-330.

Ethier, L.S., Lacharite, C. & Couture, G. (1995). Childhood adversity, parental stress and depression of negligent mothers. *Child Abuse and Neglect*, 19, 619-632.

Fantuzzo, J.W., Boruch, R., Beriama, A., Atkins, M., & Mareus, S. (1997). Domestic violence and children: Prevalence and risk in five major U.S. cites. *Journal of the American Academy of Child and Adolescent Psychiatry*, 36, 116-122.

Fantuzzo, J.W., Depalola, L.M., Lambert, L., Martino, T., Anderson, G., & Sutton, S. (1991). Effects of inter-parental violence on the psychological adjustment and competencies of young children. *Journal of Consulting and Clinical Psychology*, 59, 258-265.

Farrington, K.M. (1980). Stress and family violence. In M.A. Straus & G. T. Hataling (Eds.). *The Social causes of husband to wife violence* (pp. 94-114). Minneapolis: Flavia,A. of Minnesota Press.

Flavia, A.,(1988). "Violence in the family: Wife beating". In R. Ghadially (Ed.). *Women in Indian Society.* New Delhi: Sage.

Folkman, S. (1984). Personal control, stress and coping processes: A theoretical analysis. *Journal of Personality and Social Psychology*, 46, 839-852.

Garbarino, J. (1976). A preliminary study of some ecological correlates of child abuse: The impact of socio-economic stress on mothers. *Child Development*, 47, 178-185.

Garbarino, J., & Kostelny, K. (1992). Child maltreatment as a community problem. *Child Abuse and Neglect*, 16, 455-464.

Geffner, R.A., Jaffe, P.G. & Sudermann, M. (2000). *Children exposed to domestic violence: Current issue in research, intervention, prevention and policy development*. Binghamton, NY: Hawarth Press.

Gelles, R.J., & Straus, M.A. (1988). *Intimate violence: The definitive study of the causes and consequences of abuse in the American family*. New York: Simon and Schuster.

Ghadially, R. (ed.). 1988. *Women in Indian Society*, New Delhi: Sage.

Ghosh, S.V. (2004). Contextualizing domestic violence: Family, community, state. In R. Bhattacharya (Ed.), *Behind closed doors: Domestic violence in India*, New Delhi: Sage.

Gibbs, J. (1975). *Crime, punishment, and deterence*. New York: Elsevier.

Gil, D.G. (1971). Violence against children. *Journal of Marriage and Family*, 33, 637-648.

Gottman, J.M. (1993). *What predicts divorce*? Hillsdale, NJ: Erlbaum.

Gottman, J.M.(1979). *Marital interaction: Experimental investigations*. San Diego, CA: Academic Press.

Graham-Bermann, S.A. & Edleson, J.L. (2001). *Domestic violence in the lives of children: The future of research, intervention and social policy*. Washington, DC: American Psychological Association.

Graham-Bermann, S.A., & Levendosky, A.A. (1998). Traumatic stress symptoms in children of battered women. *Journal of Interpersonal Violence*, 13, 111-128.

Griffeths, M. (1999). Violent video games and aggression: A review of literature. *Aggression and Violent Behaviour*, 4, 203-212.

Grych, J.H., & Fincham, F.D. (1990). Marital conflict and children's adjustment: A cognitive-contextual framework. *Psychological Bulletin*, 108, 267-290.

Haynes, S.N., Follingslad, D.R., & Sullivan, J.C. (1979). Assessment of marital satisfaction and interaction. *Journal of Consulting and Clinical Psychology*, 47, 789-791.

Henning, K., Leitenberg, H., Coffey, P., Turner, T., & Bennett, R.T. (1996). Long-term psychological and social impact of witnessing physical conflict between parents. *Journal of Interpersonal Violence*, 11, 35-51.

Herrenkohl, E.C., Herrenkohl, R.C., Rupert, L.T., Egolf, B.P., & Lutz, J.G. (1995). Risk factor for behavioural dysfunction: The relative impact of maltreatment, SES, physical health problems, cognitive ability and quality of parent-child interaction. *Child Abuse and Neglect*, 19, 191-203.

Hilton, N.Z. (1992). Battered women's concerns about their children witnessing wife assault. *Journal of Interpersonal Violence*, 7, 77-86.

Hoffman—Plotkin, D., & Twentyman, C.T. (1984). A multi model assessment of behavioural and cognitive deficits in abused and neglect preschoolers. *Child Development*, 55, 794-802.

Holden, G.W., Stein, J.D., Ritchie, K.L., Harris, S.D., & Jouriles, E.N. (1998). Parenting behaviours and beliefs of battered women. In G.W. Holden, R. Geffner, & E.N. Jourlies (Eds.), *Children exposed to marital violence: Theory, research and applied issues* (pp. 289-334). Washington, DC: American Psychological Association.

Holmes, T.H., & Rahe, R.H. (1967). The social readjustment rating scale. *Journal of Psycho-somatic Research,* 11, 213-218.

Horn, J.L., & Trickett, P.K. (1998). Community violence and child development: A review of research. In P.K. Trickett & C.J. Schellenbach (Eds.), *Violence against children in the family and community,* (pp. 103-138). Washington, DC: American Psychological Association Books.

Hughes, H.M., Parkinson, D. & Vargo, M. (1989). Witnessing spouse abuse and experiencing physical abuse: A "double whammy" *Journal of Family Violence,* 4, 197-209.

Hunter, W.M., Coulter, M.L., Runyan, D.K., & Everson, M.D. (1990). Determinants of placement for sexually abused children. *Child Abuse and Neglect*, 14, 407-418.

Hurlock, E.B. (1984). *Child development*. McGraw-Hill Series in Psychology.

Jacobson, D. (1977a), 'introduction', In D. Jacobson, & S.S. Wadley (eds.,) *Women in India*. New Delhi: Manohar Publication.

Jaffe, P. G., & Geffner R. (1998). Child custody disputes and domestic violence: Critical issues for mental health, Social service and legal professionals. In G.W. Holden, R. Geffner, & E.N.E. Jouriles (Eds.), *Children exposed to marital violence: Theory, research and applied issues* (pp. 371-408). Washington, DC: American Psychological Association.

Jaffe, P.G., Lemon, N.K.D., & Poisson, S.E. (2003). *Child custody and domestic violence: A Call for safety and accountability*, U.K.: London.

Jaffe, P.G., Poisson, S.E., & Cunningham, A. (2001). Domestic violence and high-conflict divorce: Developing a new generation of research for children. In. S.A. Graham-Bermann & J.L. Edleson (Eds.), *Domestic Violence in the lives of children* (pp. 189-202). Washington, DC: American Psychological Association.

Jaffe, P.G., Wolfe, D.A., & Wilson, S.K. (1990). *Children of battered women*. Thousand Oaks, CA: Sage.

Jaffe, P., Lemon, N., Sandler, J., & Wolfe, D. (1996). *Working together to and domestic violence*, Tampa, FL: Mancorp.

Jain, D. (1975). *Indian Women*. New Delhi: Government of India.

Jejeebhoy, S.J. (1998). Wife beating in rural India. A husband's right ? Evidence from survey data. *Economic and Political Weekly* 33(15): 855-862.

Johnson, H., & Burge, V.P. (2001). Prevalence and consequences of spousal assault in Canada. *Canadian Journal of Criminology*, 43, 27-45.

Kahn & The Behavioural Health Technician Staff (1980). Wife beating and cultural context: Prevalence in the Aboriginal and Islander community in Northern Australia. *American Journal of Community Psychology*, 8, 727-731.

Kane, R.J. (2000). Police responses to restraining orders in domestic violence incidents: Identifying the custody-threshold thesis. *Criminal Justice and Behaviour*, 27, 561-580.

Karlekar, M. (1998). Domestic violence. *Economic and Political Weekly* 33(27): 1741-1751.

Kempe, C.H., Silverman, F.N., Steel, B.F., Drogemueller, W., & Silver, H.K. (1962). The bartered child syndrome. *Journal of the American Medical Association*, 17, 17-24.

Kerig, P.K., Fedorowicz, A.E., Brown, C.A., Patenaud, R.L., & Warren, M. (1998). When warriors are worriers: Gender and children's coping with interpersonal violence. *Journal of Emotional Abuse*, 1, 89-114.

King, H., Rotter,M., Calhoun, L., & Selby, J. (1978). Perceptions of the rape incident: Physicians and volunteer counselors. *Journal of Community Psychology*, 6, 74-77.

Kishwar, M. (1994). Editor Manushi. New Delhi:

Kolko, D.J. (1992). Characteristics of child victims of physical violence: Research finding & clinical implications. *Journal of Interpersonal Violence*, 7, 244-276.

Korbin, J. (1987). Child maltreatment in cross-cultural perspective: Vulnerable children and circumstances. In R.J. Gelles & J.B. Lancaster (Eds.), *Child abuse and neglect: Biosocial dimensions* (pp. 31-55). New York: Aldin de Gruyter.

Korbin, J. (1994). Socio-cultural factors in child maltreatment. In G.B., Melton & F.D. Barry (Eds.), *Protecting children from abuse and neglect. Foundations for a new national strategy*, (pp. 182-223). New York: Guilford.

Krishnan, B. (1972). Clinical psychology. In S.K. Mitra (Ed.) *A Survey of research in psychology*. Bombay: Popular Prakashan.

Krokoff, L. (1984). Anatomy of negative affect in working class marriage. *Dissertation Abstracts International*, 45, (University Microfilms No. 84-22, 109)-7A.

Kulkarni, (2000). *The Times of India*, 11-3.

Kumari, R. (1989). *Brides are not for burning: Dowry victims in India*. New Delhi: Radiant Publishers.

Kurtz, P.D., Gaudin, J.M., Howing, P.T., & Wodarski, J.S. (1993). The consequences of physical abuse and neglect on the school age child: Mediating factors . *Children and Youth Services Review*, 15, 85-104.

L.P.'S Bare Act with Short Comments (2006). *The Protection of women from domestic violence Act. 2005*, India: Law Publishers Pvt. Ltd. Allahabad.

Lazarus, R.S. (1966). *Psychological Stress and Coping Process.* New York: McGraw-Hill.

Lazarus, R., & Folkman, S. (1984). *Stress, appraisal and coping.* New York: Springer Publishing Co.

Lehman, P. (1997). The development of post traumatic stress disorder (PTSD) in a sample of child witnesses to mother assault. *Journal of Family Violence*, 12, 241-257.

Levendosky, A.A., Huth-Bocks, A.C., Semel, M.A., & Shapiro, D.L. (2002). Trauma symptoms in preschool-age children exposed to domestic violence. *Journal of Interpersonal Violence*, 17, 150-164.

Lewark, R.W., Wakefield, J.A. & Briggs, P.F. (1985). Intelligence and personality in mate choice and marital satisfaction. *Personality and Individual Differences*, 6, 471-478.

Limber, S.P., & Nation, M.A. (1998). Violence within the neighbourhood and community. In P.K. Trickett, & C.J. Schellenbach (Eds.), *Violence against children in the family and the community* (pp. 171-193). Washington DC.: American Psychological Association.

Mahadevan, K., & others (2005). Empowerment of women through health education for healthy living of mothers and children. In S. Krishna, S.K. Kumar, and V.K. Panikkar. (Eds.), *Health promotion, prevention of HIV/AIDS and Population regulation: Strategies for developing countries,* New Delhi: B.R.P.C

Mahadevan, K.(2002). *Health education for quality of life.* New Delhi, B.R.P.C.

Mahajan, A. (1990). Instigators of wife battering. In Sooshma Sood (Ed.), *Violence against women.* Jaipur: Arihant Publishers.

Mandelbaum, D.G. (1949).The Family in India. In Ruth Anshen (Ed.), *The Family.* New York: Harper and Row.

Markman, H.J. & Notarins, C.I. (1987). Coding marital and family in interaction: Current status. In T. Jacob (Ed.). *Family interaction and psychopathology: Theories, methods and findings* (pp. 329-390). New York: Plenum Press.

Mc Closkey, L., Figueredo, A., & Koss, M. (1995). The effects of systematic family violence on children's mental health. *Child Development*, 66, 1239-1261.

Mc Farlane, J., Parker, B., Soeken, K. & Bullock, L. (1992). Assessing for abuse during pregnancy: Severity and frequency of injuries and associated entry into prenatal care. *Journal of the American Medical Association*, 267, 3176-3178.

McGrath, J.E., (Ed.) (1970). *Social psychological factors in stress*, New York: Holt, Reinchart & Winsten.

McLoyd, V.C. (1998). Socio-economic disadvantage and child development. *American Psychologist*, 53, 185-204.

Milner, J.S. (1998). Individual and family characteristics associated with interfamilial child physical and sexual abuse. In P.K. Trickett & C.J. Schellenbach (Eds.), *Violence against children in the family and community* (pp. 141-170). Washington, D.C., American Psychological Association.

Milner, J.S., & Chilamkurti, C. (1991). Physical child abuse perpetrator characteristics: A review of the literature. *Journal of Interpersonal Violence*, 6, 336-344.

Milner, J.S., Halsey, L.B. & Fultz, J. (1995). Empathic responsiveness and affective reactivity to infant in high and low risk for physical child abuse mothers. *Child Abuse and Neglect*, 19, 776-780.

Mishra, R. (2006). *Report on domestic violence in Uttar Pradesh. Danik Jagaran*, India: U.P.

Misra, G., & Tripathi, L.B. (1980). *Psychological consequences of prolonged deprivation*. Agra: National Psychological Corporation.

Mitchell, R., & Hodson, C. (1983). Coping with domestic violence: Social support and psychological health among battered women. *American Journal of Community Psychology*, 11, 629-654.

Mitra, N. (2006). Best practices among responses to domestic violence in Maharashtra and Madhya Pradesh. In N. Duvvury (Project Director) ICRW, *Domestic violence in India: A Summary Report*, U.S.A.: Washingfon, DC.

Moore, T.E., Pepler, D., Mae, R., & Michele, K. (1989). Effects of family violence on children: New directions for research and intervention. In B. Pressman & G. Cameron (Eds.), *Interviewing with assaulted women: Current theory research, and practice* (pp. 75-91). Hillsdale, NJ: Lawrence Erlbaum Associates.

Nanda, B.R. (1976*). Indian women*, New Delhi: Vikas.

Narayana, G. (1996) "Family violence, sex and reproductive health behaviour among men in Uttar Pradesh. India": *The Futures Group*.

National Academy of Sciences (1993). *Understanding child abuse and neglect*. Washington, D.C.: National Academy Press.

Olson, D.H., Spengle, D.H., & Russell, C.S. (1979). Circumplex model of marital and family systems: Cohesion and adaptability dimensions, family types, and clinical applications. *Family Process*, 18, 3-28.

Paik, H., & Comstock, G. (1994). The effects of television violence on antisocial behaviour: A meta-analysis. *Communication Research*, 21, 516-546.

Pandey, S. (2001a). Role of empowerment and future orientation in family planning behaviour. In Frank. Trovato et al. (Eds.) *Health Strategies and Population Regulation*, Vol. (3). New Delhi: BRPC.

Pandey, S. (2001b). Changing perception and attitude towards dowry: An emperical study. *Indian Journal of Psychological issues,* 9, 45-50.

Pandey, S.(2005). Child abuse: An impediment to the development of creative potential in children. Psychological Studies, 15, 234-242.

Pandey, S. (2006). *Personal data sheet (P.D.S.).* Report submitted to N.C.W. unpublished research project. Department of Psychology. D.S.A., D.D.U. Gorakhpur University, Gorakhpur.

Pandey, S., & Mishra, B. (2000). Dowry and status of women in India. In K. Mahadevan, GAO Ersheng, Yu Jing Yuan, R. Jayasree, A.K.M. Nurun Nabi, P. Rajaram, F. Bourdier, P.J. Reddy, V.K.R. Kumar, & V.M. Sandeep (Eds.), *Reproductive health of humankind in Asia and Africa: A global perspective;* New Delhi: B.R.P.C

Pandey, S., & Srivastava, S. (2004). Role of coping in work stress-health relationship: A study on career women. A. Husain & Rashid (Eds.). *Stress Behaviour: The Coping Strategies*, Vol. 2, New Delhi: Friends Publication.

Pati, G.C. (1976). *Aggression Questionnaire*, Rupa Psychological Center, Varanasi.

Perkins, D.D., & Zimmerman, M.A. (1995). Empowerment theory, research, and application. An introduction to a special issue. *American Journal of Community Psychology*, 23, 569-579.

Perry, B.D. (1995). Incubated in terror: Neurodevelopmental factors in the cycle of violence. In J.D. Osofsky (Ed.), *Children, youth and violence: Searching for solutions*. New York: Guilford Press.

Pestonjee, D.M. (1992). *Stress and coping*. New Delhi: Sage.

Poonacha, V. & Pandey, D. (2006). Responses to domestic violence in Karnataka and Gujarat. In N. Duvvury (Project Director; ICRW), *Domestic violence in India: A summary report*. U.S.A.: Washington, D.C.

Prino, C.T., & Peyrot, M. (1994). The effect of child physical abuse and neglect on aggressive, withdrawn, and pro-social behaviour. *Child Abuse and Neglect*, 18, 871-884.

Putt, J., & Higgins, K. (1997). *Violence against women in Australia*. Griffith ACT: Australian Institute of Criminology.

Randolf, M., & Talamo, Y. (1997). Multi-method evaluation of children who witness domestic violence. *Poster Presented at the Second International Conference on Children Exposed to Domestic Violence,* London, ON.

Rao, V.V.P., & Rao, V.N. (1982) *Marriage, the family and women in India*, Columbia, Missouri: South Asian Books.

Rao, V. (1996). Wife beating in rural South India: A qualitative and economic analysis. *Social Science Medicine* 00(0): 1-12.

Rappaport, J. (1984). Studies in empowerment: Introduction to issue. *Prevention in Human Services*, 3, 1-7.

Raush, H.L., Barry, W.A., Hertel, R.K. & Swain, M.A. (1974). *Communication, conflict and marriage*. San Francisco: Jossey Bass.

Reitzel, J.D. & Wolfe, D.A. (2001). Predictions of relationship abuse among young men. *Journal of Interpersonal Violence*, 16, 99-115.

Rennison, C.M., & Welchans, S. (2000). *Bureau of Justice statistics special report: Intimate partner violence.* Washington, DC: U.S. Department of Justice.

Resick, P., & Jackson, T. (1981). Attitudes toward rape among mental health professionals. *American Journal of Community Psychology*, 9, 481-490.

Riger, S., Gordon, M., & Le Bailly, R. (1982). Coping with urban crime: Women's use of precautionary behaviours. *American Journal of Community Psychology*, 10, 369-386.

Rodgers, K. (1994). *Wife assault: The findings of a national survey* (Rep. no. juristat 14:9).

Rosenberg, M.S., & Reppucci, N.D. (1985). Primary prevention of child abuse. *Journal of Consulting and Clinical Psychology*, 53, 576-585.

Rossman, B.B.R., Hughes, H.M., & Rosenberg, M.S. (2000). *Children and inter-parental violence: The impact of exposure.* Philadelphia: Brunner/Mazel.

Rudo, Z.H., Powell, D.S., & Dunlap, G. (1998). The effects of violence in the home on children's emotional, behavioural and social functioning: A review of the literature. *Journal of Emotional and Behavioural Disorders*, 6, 94-113.

Rutter, M. (1979). Protective factors in children's responses to stress and disadvantage. In M. W. Kent & J. E. Roff (Eds.). *Primary prevention of psychopathology, social competence in children* (pp. 49-74). Hanover, N H: University Press of New England.

Rutter, M. (1983) 'Stress, coping and development in children: Some issues and some questions'. In N. Garmezy & M. Rutter (Eds.). *Stress, coping and development in children.* New York: McGraw-Hill.

Schteingart, J.S., Molnar, J., Klein, T.P., Lowe, C.B. & Hartman, A.H. (1995). Homelessness and child functioning in the context of risk and protective factors moderating child outcomes. *Journal of Clinical Child Psychology*, 24, 320-331.

Schuler, R.S. (1980). A role and expectancy perception model of participation in decision making, *Academy of Management Journal*, 23, 331-340.

Sedlak, A.J., & Broadhurst, D.D. (1996). *Executive summary of the third National Incidence Study of child abuse and neglect.* (DHHS Pub. No. ACF-105-94-1840). Washington, D.C.; Government Parenting Office.

Seligman, C., Bush, M. & Krisch, K. (1975). Relationship between compliance in the foot-in the door paradigm and size of first request. *Journal of Personality and Social Psychology*, 33, 517-520.

Selye, H. (1956). *The Stress of life*. New York: McGraw-Hill.

Shields, A.M., Cicchetti, D., & Ryan, R.M. (1994). The development of emotional and behavioural self-regulation and social competence among maltreated school age children. *Development and Psychopathology*, 6, 57-75.

Simonelli, C.J., Mullis, T., Elliott, A.N., & Pierce, T.W. (2002). Abuse by siblings and subsequent experiences of violence within the dating relationship. *Journal of Interpersonal Violence*, 17, 103-121.

Sims, B., Hans, S., & Cox, S. (1996). Raising children in high-risk environments: Mother's experience of stress and distress related to attachment security. Poster presented at the biennial meeting of the International Conference on Infant Studies, Providence, RI. This research is reported in J. Cassidy & P.R. Shaver, (Eds.). (1999). *Handbook of attachment: Theory, research and applications* (p. 257). New York: Guilford Press.

Smolen, R.C., Spiegel, D.A., & Martin, C.J. (1986). Patterns of marital interaction associated with marital dissatisfaction and depression. *Journal of Behaviour Therapy and Experimental Psychiatry*, 17, 261-266.

Spence, J., & Helmreich, R. (1978). *Masculinity and Feminity, Their psychological dimensions, correlates and antecedents.* Austin: University of Taxes Press.

Sroufe, L.A. (1989). Pathways to adaptation and maladaptation: Psychopathology as development deviation. In D. Cicchetti (Ed.), *Rochester Symposium on developmental psychopathology: Vol. 1. The emergence of a discipline* (pp. 13-40). Hullsdale, NJ: Lawrence Erlbaum.

Stagg, V., Wills, G.D., & Howell, M. (1989). Psychopathology in early childhood witnesses of family violence. *Topics in Early Childhood Special Education*, 9, 73-87.

Sternberg, K.J., Lamb, M.E., Greenbaum, C., Cicchetti, D., Dawrd, S., Cortes, R.M., Krispin, O., & Lorey, F. (1993). Effects of domestic Violence on children's behaviour problems and depression. *Developmental Psychology*, 29, 44-52.

Straus, M.A. (1977). *Societal morphogenesis and intrafamily violence in cross-cultural perspective*. Annals of the New York: Academy of Science, 285-717-730.

Straus, M.A. (1992). Children as witnesses to marital violence: A risk factor for lifelong problems among a nationally representative sample of American men and women. In. D.F. Schwarz (Ed.), *Children and violence: Report on the 23rd Ross Roundtable on, critical approaches to common pediatric problems* (pp. 98-104). Columbus, OH: Ross Laboratories.

Straus, M.A. Gelles, R.J., & Steinmetz, S.K. (1980). *Behind closed doors: Violence in the American family.* Beverly Hills, C.A.: Sage.

Straus, M.A., & Gelles, R.J. (Eds.) (1990). *Physical violence in American families*. New Brunswick, N.J.: Transaction Books.

Swift, C., & Levin, G. (1987). Empowerment: An emerging mental health technology. *Journal of Primary Prevention*, 7, 242-263.

Terman, L.M., Butterweiser, P., Ferguson, L.W., Johnson, W.B., & Wilson, D.P. (1938). *Psychological factors in marital happiness* New York: McGraw-Hill.

Thompson, R.A. (1994). Social support and the prevention of child maltreatment. In G.B. Metton & Barry (Eds.). *Protecting children from abuse and neglect: Foundations for new national strategy* pp. 40-130). New York: Guilford.

Times of India, (2006). Lucknow Edition.

Tjaden, P., & Thoennes, N. (2000). *Full report of the prevalence incidence, and consequences of violence against women: Findings from the national violence against women survey*. Washington, DC: U.S. Department of Justice, Office of Justice Programs.

Tolan, P.H. & Guerra, N. (1998) Societal causes of violence against children. In P.K. Trickett & C.J. Schellenbach (Eds.), *Violence against children in the family and the community*, (pp. 195-209). Washington DC: American Psychological Association.

Trickett, P.K., Alber, J.L., Carlson, V., & Cicchetti, D. (1991). Relationship of socio-economic status to the etiology and developmental sequelae of physical child abuse. *Developmental Psychology*, 27, 148-158.

Vincent, J.P., & Friedman, L.C. (1979). Demand characteristics in observation of marital interaction. *Journal of Consulting and Clinical Psychology*, 47, 557-566.

Vincent, J.P., Weiss, R.L., & Birchler, G.R. (1975). A behavioural analysis of problem solving in distressed and non-distressed married and stranger dyads. *Behaviour Therapy*, 6, 475-489.

Visario, L. (1999). Violence against women in India: Evidence from rural Gujarat. In N. Duvvury (Project Director ICRW) *Domestic violence in India: A summary report*, U.S.A.; Washington, D.C.

W.H.O. Report, (2006). Prevalence rate of violence in various countries. *World Health Organization Report*, Geneva.

Walker, L.E. (1979). *The battered woman*, New York: Harper and Row.

Walker, L., Thompson, N., & Lindsay, W. (1984). 'Assessing family relationships: A multi-method, multi-situational approach'. *British Journal of Psychiatry*, 144, 387-394.

Ward, C., & Sethi, R. (1983). 'Cross-cultural validation of Bem's sex role inventory: Malaysian and South Indian Research' Paper presented at *Third Asian Regional Conference of International Association of Cross-Cultural Psychology*, Bangi Malaysia.

Weiss, R.L., & Summers, K.J. (1983). Marital interaction coding system 111. In E.E. Filsinger (Ed.), *Marriage and family assessment*, (pp. 85-120). Beverly Hills, CA: Sage.

Weithorn, L.A. (2001). Protecting children from exposure to domestic violence: The use and abuse of child maltreatment status. *Hastings Law Journal*, 53, 1-56.

Welford, A.T. (1973). Stress and performance, *Ergonomics*, 16, 567.

William, L.M., & Finkelhar, D. (1990). The characteristics of incestuous fathers: A review of recent studies. In W.L. Marshall, D.R. Lawss and H.E. Barbaree (Eds.). *Handbook of sexual assault: Issue, theories and treatment of the offender* (pp. 231-255) New York: Plenum.

Williams, J.E., & Best, D. (1982). *Measuring sex stereotypes: A thirty nation study*. Newbury Park, California: Sage.

Wolfe, D., Werkele, C., Reitzel-Jaffe, D., & Lefebvere, L. (1998). Factors associated with abusive relationship among maltreated and non-maltreated youth. *Development and Psychopathology*, 10, 61-85.

Wolfgang, M.E., & Ferracuti, F. (1972). *Delinquency in a birth cohort*. London: Tavistock.

Wolman, B. (Ed.) (1973). *Dictionary of behavioural sciences*. New York: Van Mostrand.

World Health Organization, (2002). *World report on violence and health. Times of India.*

Wyatt, G.E. (1994). Socio-cultural and epidemiological issues in the assessment of domestic violence. *Journal of Social Distress and the Homeless*, 3, 7-21.

Yogev, S. (1986). Relationships between stress and marital satisfaction among dual-earner couples. *Women and Therapy*, 5, 313-330.

Zahn-Waxler, C., Cole, P.M., Welsh, J.D., & Fox, N.A. (1995). Psychological correlates of empathy and prosocial behaviours in preschool children with behaviour problems. *Development of Psychopathology*, 7, 27-48.

Zimmerman, M. A., Ramirez-Valles, J., Suarez, E., de la Rosa, G., & Castro, M. A. (1997). *An HIV/AIDS prevention project for Mexican homosexual men: An empowerment approach. Health Education and Behavio*ur, 24, 177-190.

Index